HOW THE BAHAMAS & TURKS AND CAICOS ISLANDS Got Their Names

(A companion book to the trilogy titled The Lucayan Sea: A Case for Naming the Historic Waters of The Bahamas & The Turks and Caicos Islands)

TELLIS A. BETHEL SR.

Copyrights

ISBN: 9798401236944
Publisher: Inspire Publishing, The Bahamas

www.Inspirepublishing.org

Cover Design: Teri M. Bethel

Books written under the series titled *Lucayan Sea: A Case for Naming the Historic Waters of The Bahamas & Turks and Caicos Islands* may be ordered through booksellers and Amazon.com.

Dedication

To the many visitors who travel to our shores aboard commercial and private airlines, yachts, boats, and cruise lines to explore and experience our beautiful islands, friendly people, and pristine waters. This book is also dedicated to those employed in the travel and tourism industry within these islands and overseas, helping our visitors enjoy the best our islands offer.

Table of Contents

Illustrations

Illustration 1: Map of the Lucayan Archipelago

Illustration 2: An artist's rendition of Christopher Columbus during his first voyage

Illustration 3: 1764 'Carte des isles situées au nord de St. Domingue'

Illustration 4: Spanish Americas during the 1600s

Illustration 5: A dissection of Antonio de Herrera y Tordesillas'1601 map displaying Grand Bahama as Bahama Island.

Illustration 6: Arawak Indian village in South America

Illustration 7: An artist's rendition of Christopher Columbus' landfall on San Salvador Island

Illustration 8: Map of San Salvador Island, Bahamas

Illustration 9: Antonio de Herrera y Tordesillas' 1601 map showing the Lucayan Islands

Illustration 10. A dissection of Spanish Cartographer and navigator Juan de la Cosa's 1500 world map

Photos

Acknowledgments

I'm appreciative of the historians, archaeologists, and other scholars who have worked tirelessly in documenting and publishing their research on The Bahamas and Turks and Caicos Islands. And to the invaluable efforts of The Bahamas National Trust and The Bahamas Antiquities, Monuments and Museums Corporation, the Bahamas Historical Society, the Turks and Caicos National Museum, and other nonprofit organizations in preserving and promoting our islands' natural heritage.

Terminologies & Pronunciations

Throughout this series, references are made to such terms as the "New World," "the Americas," "the birthplace of the Americas," "the Lucayan Islands," "the Lucayan Archipelago," and "the modern era," and others. These terminologies are explained below to bring clarity to the context in which they are presented.

Pronunciations

Before outlining the terminologies used in this series, there are three keywords that some readers may want to know how to pronounce. These words are Lucayan, Bahamian, and Caicos.

Lucayan is pronounced: **Lu** (as in **Lu**ke)-**kay** (as in **kay**ak)-**an** (as in Puerto Ri**can**).

Bahamian is pronounced: **Ba** (as in **Bah**rain)-**ham** (as in low sounding **h+aim** or **haim**; the ian (as in the Japanese **yen**)

Caicos: Cai (as in the letter **K**)-cos (as in **cus**tomer or as in **cost**)

The Ancient World of the Western Hemisphere:

It is widely believed that the continents and islands of the Western Hemisphere were initially settled by Asian peoples and their descendants thousands of years before European arrival. There were no collective names for the Western

Hemisphere's continents and archipelagos at the time of the Americas' founding. Although early inhabitants had indigenous names for their ethnic groups, they were often referred to as Amerindians, Aborigines, Native Americans, Indigenous Peoples, or the First Nations, Inuit, and Métis peoples of Canada by Europeans and their descendants. Some of these terminologies are used in this series.

Readers should also note that the name "Americas" never existed until the early 1500s. Consequently, the term "Ancient World of the Western Hemisphere" (or Ancient World in its shortened form) is used in reference to the Western Hemisphere's mainland (the northern and southern continents), islands (circum-Caribbean region and the Lucayan Islands), associated waters, and the indigenous peoples who inhabited these lands before European contact in 1492.

The Lucayan Islands:

"The Lucayan Islands" constitute an archipelago whose northern end is near the southeastern limits of the United States, and its southern boundary is near the northern coasts of the Republic of Haiti and the Dominican Republic on the island of Hispaniola in the northern Caribbean (the Greater Antilles). The Lucayan Archipelago is geographically separated from the United States and the Caribbean.

The Lucayan people are descendants of the Taino people in the northern Caribbean (Greater Antilles), who originally inhabited the Lucayan Archipelago before the Lucayan culture was formed. Today, the archipelago comprises the independent country of the Commonwealth of The Bahamas and the British Overseas Territory of the Turks and Caicos Islands at the island chain's southeastern end.[1]

Whenever the term "Lucayan Islands" or "Lucayan Archipelago" is used in this series, it refers to both the Bahama Islands (The Bahamas) and the Turks and Caicos Islands. When addressing the two territories as politically separated archipelagos, the Bahama Islands is referred to as the Bahama Archipelago, and the Turks and Caicos Islands as the Turks and Caicos Islands Archipelago.

The Modern Era (or Modern History):

"The modern era" is a term that describes the period between 1492 to the present time. This period indicates the beginning of a new era in human history,[2] including the Ancient World of the Western Hemisphere. For Europeans, 1492 was the closing chapter of the Middle Ages (or the medieval period) and the onset of the modern age.[3] The Middle Ages generally refers to the period starting with Rome's fall (476 BC) to the Renaissance Period, which some propose began during the 13th, 14th, or 15th centuries.[4]

Spain sometimes refers to 1492 as the end of the Middle Ages and the beginning of the modern era.[5] This series identifies the year of Columbus' landfall in the Ancient World (1492) as the closing chapter for the Ancient World of the Western Hemisphere and the beginning of the modern era for the Americas—politically, economically, and culturally.

The "New World" Concept:

The title "New World" was a concept created by Europeans who had a Eurocentric mindset about the world. The Ancient World was "new" to Old World Europeans after Columbus happened upon it. These explorers had no prior knowledge of the Ancient World's existence at the onset of the modern era. However, the Ancient World was not "new" to the Western Hemisphere's indigenous peoples, nor was it "discovered" by Europeans, as indeed it was inhabited by indigenous peoples for thousands of years before European contact.

The Old World of Europe

The term "Old World" generally refers to those continents and peoples on the Atlantic Ocean's eastern side (Europe, Asia, Africa, and Australia).[6] For this book's purposes, the term Old World of Europe is applied to those European countries that colonized the Ancient World after 12 October 1492, resulting in what is now known as the Americas. These countries included Spain, Portugal, England, France, and the (Dutch) Netherlands.

The Americas:

The name Americas is an Old World description of the islands and continents that European explorers encountered in the Ancient World. European cartographers introduced this name at the beginning of a modern era for the Americas during the early 1500s. In this series, the term "Americas" or the "Wider Americas" generally refers to today's North, South, and Central America, and the circum-Caribbean region (including the Lucayan Islands), and associated waters within the Western Hemisphere.

The New World of the Americas:

Although initially "new" to early Europeans after Columbus' first landfall in the Ancient World of the Western Hemisphere, the Ancient World was gradually transformed into a new one politically, economically, culturally, and socially. This transformation began on 12 October 1492, the day Columbus arrived in the Lucayan Islands during his first voyage, beginning the Old World's exploration, exploitation, and colonization of the Ancient World. It was not until the early 1500s that European cartographers named the Ancient World "America."

As a result, this series describes the post-1492 Ancient World as the "New World of the Americas," which consists of the nations that emerged due to the permanent reunion of two main branches of civilization (the Ancient World and the Old World) during the modern era. In the context of this series, the term New World of the Americas does not necessarily apply to those territories inhabited or administered by today's descendants of the indigenous peoples.

Currently, the United Nations (U.N.) acknowledges over 30 sovereign nations in the Western Hemisphere. Territories controlled by indigenous groups within these sovereign nations are not identified as sovereign states by the U.N. Over the years, the Americas has become a melting pot of the Ancient World indigenous peoples and descendants of the Old World peoples (Africans, Europeans, and Asians).

Today, the Americas consists of over 33 modern nations, some of which have allocated lands to descendants of native peoples from the Ancient World to administrate and develop. These territorial allotments include Indian Reservations in the United States, The Toronto Purchase in Canada,[7] and the Kalinago Territory in the Commonwealth of Dominica, managed by state-recognized tribes. Nevertheless, much of the indigenous traditions, ways, customs, tribes, and empires were destroyed by the European invasion of the hemisphere, and new nations were born.

The Birthplace of the Americas:

The waters surrounding the Lucayan Archipelago became the gateway for European access to the Ancient World. The events that followed resulted in the Americas' founding and the unfolding of the Americas' modern nations. Therefore, the Lucayan waters surrounding The Bahamas and Turks and Caicos Islands (the Lucayan Archipelago) are described as the "Birthplace of the Americas" (or the "Birthplace of the New World of the Americas") in this series.

xvii

The Site Where the Americas were Founded:

"The site where the Americas were founded" refers to the Lucayan Archipelago, where Columbus first arrived and made landfall in the Ancient World in 1492. It was from this site that the modern nations of the Americas unfolded.

Heritage:

The word "heritage" describes the history and geography of an island (or a country) and the culture its people inherited or passed down to successive generations. "History" refers to past events, including political, economic, and social affairs. "Geography" describes the land and sea and an island's natural resources and physical features (or country).

"Culture" is defined as a people's way of life, including customs and traditions. In this series, a national heritage is considered those dimensions of history, geography, and culture beneficial to fulfilling national interests and advancing humanity's longevity, prosperity, and security.

Spaniards and Spanish:

The terms Spaniard or Spanish apply to people, places, or things originating from or related to Spain unless otherwise stated.

Introduction

The names "Bahamas" and "Turks and Caicos Islands" resonate loud and clear in the minds of millions around the world. These names are synonymous with the friendly people and turquoise waters of an island paradise north of the Caribbean Islands and east of Florida. With over half a billion combined name-related searches on Google's search engine, millions visit these islands annually to experience a vacation of a lifetime. Untold numbers also enjoy these islands and their breath-taking waters through print and electronic media.

The Bahamas and Turks and Caicos Islands are collectively called the Lucayan Islands. The Lucayan Islands' waters mark the spot where the Old World of Europe encountered the ancient world of the Western Hemisphere (now called the Americas) after Italian explorer Christopher Columbus made his first landfall in this part of the world on Lucayan shores in 1492. Subsequent events transformed the Ancient World of the Western Hemisphere into the New World of the Americas, making these islands' waters the birthplace of the Americas.

Photo 1: Spanish Galleon (Source: Wikimedia. By Miriam Thyes)

Before European contact, The Bahamas and Turks and Caicos Islands did not exist as separate territories within the same island chain, nor were these islands inhabited by different ethnic groups when Columbus arrived. However, each island had an indigenous name and was settled by an ethnic group called Lukku Cairi (or Lucayan in its English form). Spanish colonists in the northern Caribbean Islands captured and exported the enslaved Lucayans to neighboring Caribbean Islands during the late 1400s and early1500s.

By 1530, the Lucayan Islands were believed to be depopulated and remained uninhabited for over 100 years. English colonists from Bermuda resettled the islands during the latter half of the 1600s. Today, The Bahamas and Turks and Caicos Islands are politically separated countries inhabited chiefly by people of African ancestry. The two countries have since emerged through colonization and slavery to become premier tourist destinations and leading offshore financial centers within the Caribbean region.

Despite these islands' rich heritage, inquiring minds often overlook intriguing details of how The Bahamas and the Turks and Caicos Islands got their names. The enlightening story behind these names would fascinate the imaginations of those who enjoy discovering fresh insights about these islands' extraordinary heritage and their influence on the Americas' founding.

Insights documented in this book were derived from geographical features, old nautical charts, and cultural perspectives relevant to these islands. This writer also examined the early Spanish language and the impact Spanish mariners had on The Bahamas' and the Turks and Caicos Islands' names.

Additionally, this writer's experiences as a former naval officer in the Royal Bahamas Defence Force were also considered in determining how The Bahamas and Turks and Caicos Islands got their names. Admittedly, research on the origins of The Bahamas' name was more challenging than finding out how the Turks and Caicos Islands got their names.

Although this companion book focuses mainly on how the names of each country came about, readers should note that more details about The Bahamas' and Turks and Caicos Islands' history and geography are found in Books 1 and 2 of the trilogy *The Lucayan Sea: A Case for Naming the Historic Waters of The Bahamas and Turks and Caicos Islands*. Books 1 and 2 are titled *The Lucayan Islands and The Lucayan Sea—The Birthplace of the Americas*.

How *The Bahamas & Turks and Caicos Islands Got Their Names*, was written to bring about a greater appreciation for these islands' rich heritage among Bahamians, Turks and Caicos Islanders, and their residents. It is also hoped that the story behind these countries' names would create a more memorable and meaningful experience for those who visit these shores.

Chapter 1

A Brief History

The Bahamas and Turks and Caicos Islands make up the Lucayan Archipelago. An archipelago is a chain or group of islands surrounded by a common body of water. The Lucayan Archipelago consists of over 700 islands in a maritime domain stretching northwest to southeast for about 700 miles (1,126 km). The Bahama Islands extend the entire length of this archipelagic chain from Abaco Island at its northern end to Inagua Island at its southern end. Grand Bahama Island is in the northwestern part of the island chain and about 60 miles (96 km) east of Palm Beach on South Florida's east coast.

The Turks and Caicos Islands are a tiny group of islands near the southeastern end of the Lucayan Archipelago. *Its nearest inhabited island (Providenciales) is* approximately 50 miles (80 km) northeast of The Bahamas' southern-most island, Great Inagua Island. Salt Cay is the Turks and Caicos Islands' southernmost inhabited landmass. The cay is about 100 miles (160 km) north of the Dominican Republic and almost 120 miles (193 km) east of Great Inagua Island, the Bahamas' southernmost island.

The Lucayan Islands were initially settled by the Lucayan people, whose ancestors occupied these islands from around

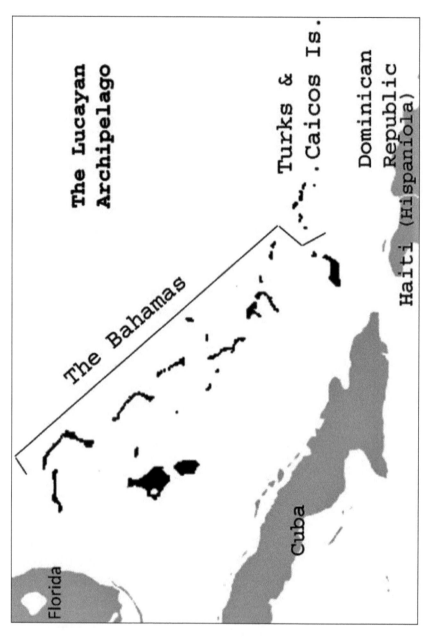

Illustration 1: Map of the Lucayan Archipelago (Source: Wikipedia, Names inserted)

700 AD[8] (or earlier by some accounts). About eight centuries after settling the Lucayan Islands, Italian explorer Christopher Columbus stumbled upon the islands on 12 October 1492 while en route to the East Indies. Here in these islands, Columbus was warmly received by the Lucayans.

The friendly Lucayans were the original permanent inhabitants of the Lucayan Islands at European contact. Columbus made his first landfall in the Ancient World of the Western Hemisphere on a tiny island the indigenous Lucayans called Guanahani in the central Bahamas. Columbus renamed the island San Salvador and claimed it for the Spanish Crown, believing he had arrived in the East Indies.

The historic encounter between the Old World of Europe and the Ancient World of the Western Hemisphere initiated the most dramatic events in the Americas at the beginning of the modern era, forever changing world history. Having originated from the Lucayan Archipelago, these events made the Lucayan Islands' waters the geographical womb from which the Americas' modern nations came.

Illustration 2: *An artist's rendition of Christopher Columbus during his first voyage by Carl von Piloty. (Source: Wikipedia)*

Though Columbus made three more trips to the Americas from Spain, he never returned to the Lucayan Islands. However, Spain and its European rivals dominated the natives and their lands throughout the Western Hemisphere during the centuries that followed Columbus' historic voyage. European territorial claims and conquests are reflected in the names European powers gave their conquered lands and regions, such as Florida, Argentina, the Antilles, and the Americas. The Spanish called the Lucayan chain of islands Las Islas de Los Lucayos (or Las Lucayas).[9]

The Spaniards conquered and colonized the northern Caribbean Islands (or the Greater Antilles) in their quest for gold. Due to the rapid depletion of the indigenous Taino slave labor in the northern Caribbean Islands, Spanish ships were sent on slave-raiding expeditions in the Lucayan Islands as early as 1499, according to early historical records.[10] Within 30 to 40 years of Columbus' arrival, the entire Lucayan population (an estimated minimum of 20,000[11] to 40,000[12] Lucayans) was wiped out.

The Lucayans were captured and exported to Hispaniola, Cuba, and Puerto Rico, where they worked as enslaved people in the gold mines and plantations of these north Caribbean Islands. Most Lucayans died from European diseases, brutal slave treatment, hunger, and suicide. Many were also shipped as far south as Cubagua, an island off the northeast coast of Venezuela in the Caribbean, where the Spanish worked them to death as skilled oyster pearl divers.[13]

Bermudan colonists from England resettled the abandoned Lucayan Islands about 125 years after the Lucayan extinction. In 1647, an English group called the Eleutheran Adventurers was granted rights to establish the Plantation of Eleuthera on the Island of Eleuthera in the central Bahamas. The recolonization of the Bahama Islands began in Eleuthera in 1648, making Eleuthera the birthplace of the modern Bahamas.

About 30 years later, a separate group of Bermudans began resettling the Turks and Caicos Islands at the southern end of the Lucayan Island chain during the 1670s. These Bermudans eventually developed a lucrative salt industry in the Turks and Caicos Islands. The enterprise was vital for preserving food in British colonies on the North American mainland, the Caribbean Islands, and aboard merchant vessels.

The Bahama Colony's demand for the Turks and Caicos Islands to pay taxes on monies made from the Turks and Caicos Island's "white gold" (salt) industry provoked an administrative scuffle between the two colonies. Contention between the two groups resulted in The Bahama Colony being granted administrative control over the Turks and Caicos Islands on at least three occasions (1766, 1848, and 1962).

In 1848, the Turks and Caicos Islands was separated from the Bahama Colony and granted self-governance under Jamaica's supervision by Great Britain. Nevertheless, the Turks and Caicos Islands was returned under the Bahama Colony's administrative rule after the Jamaica Colony was granted independence by Great Britain in 1962.[14]

The identification of the Turks and Caicos Islands as two distinct island groups (the Turks Islands group and the Caicos Islands group) continued until 1848, when British authorities placed the colony under a single name, the Turks and Caicos Islands.[15] The Bahamas and Turks and Caicos Islands were permanently separated (politically) after the Bahama Colony gained its independence from Great Britain on 10 July 1973. After that, the Turks and Caicos Islands became a Crown Colony with an appointed Governor. Today, the Turks and Caicos Islands is a British Overseas Territory.

Chapter 2

Origin of the Names "Turks Islands" and "Caicos Islands"

As indicated in Chapter 1, the Turks and Caicos Islands comprise two main groups of islands: the Turks and the Caicos groups. The 22-mile (35 km) wide Turks Passage, also known as the Columbus Passage, separates the two groups. The Turks group is on the east side of the passage and consists of Grand Turk and Salt Cay, some 11 miles (17 km) south of Grand Turks. The Caicos group is on the western side of the Turks Passage and includes North, South, East, West, and Middle Caicos Islands and Providenciales.

The French hydrographer Jacques Nicolas Bellin's 1764 map displays Grand Turk and Salt Cay as Grande Saline (Big Salt) and Petit Saline (Small Salt). The Caicos group is collectively named Les Cayques (The Caicos). West Caicos is named Petite Caique (Small Caicos). Providenciales is unnamed. North, Middle, East Caicos, and South Caicos were identified as Cayque du Nord au La Grande Cayque (Caicos from North to Big Caicos). The 1764 map was published two years before the British Crown formally claimed the islands in 1766.[16]

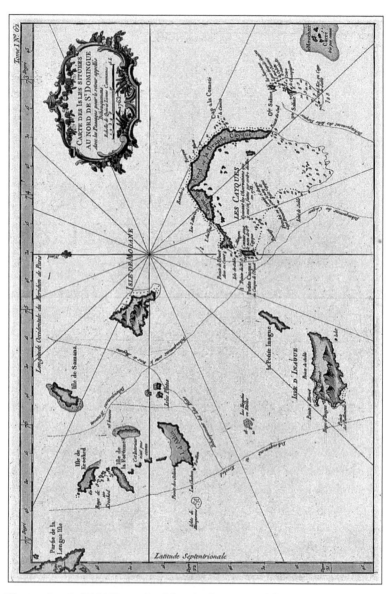

Illustration 3: 1764 'Carte des isles situées au nord de St. Domingue' Map by French Hydrographer Jacques Nicolas Bellin. This map displays the Turks and Caicos Islands in the lower right-hand (southeast) section of the map. (Source: Wikimedia).

Photo 2: The Turks Head (or Turks Cap Cactus) Plant. (Source: By Wilfredor, Wikimedia)

The name "Turks" is believed to have come from an indigenous cactus plant found in the Turks and Caicos Islands called the Turk's Head (or the *Melocactus intortus* species). The fruit on top of the plant is eaten by lizards, iguanas, and people.[17]

The plant is also known as the Turks Cap Cacti and can grow up to 24 inches (61 centimeters) tall and 14 inches (35 centimeters) in diameter. It is said that the scarlet-topped cactus plant reminded European mariners of the Turkish fez—a hat commonly worn by men in Turkey. The island eventually became synonymous with the Turks from Turkey.[18]

Another theory is that the name Turks came about due to pirates who loitered near the Turks Islands' coasts. The pirates waited to attack and pillage Spanish treasure ships en route to

13

Spain from the Old Bahama Channel during the 17th and 18th centuries. These pirates were reminiscent of the pirates of the Ottoman Empire founded by Turkish tribes. Ironically, Ottoman pirates were robbing European ships in the Mediterranean while Europeans raided indigenous lands in the Americas, shipping their stolen treasure to Spain. For some, the name Turks Island is interpreted as meaning "Pirate Island."[19]

While several theories exist concerning the origin of Turks Island's name, Caicos is easily traced to its indigenous inhabitants. It is believed that the name Caicos was derived from the Taino words "cayo hico,"[20] and has two meanings.

One meaning is "string of islands,"[21] suggesting that the Lucayans might have identified several islands in the Caicos group using a single name. However, the other meaning is "outer" or "far away island."[22] The indigenous name "Caicos" was later published on European maps that were widely circulated, and the name remains in use today.[1]

Regardless of the theories behind the name Turks, this name appears to be of European origin, but Caicos is a Taino name. The origins of both names ("Turks" and "Caicos") help tell the story of their indigenous inhabitants and European explorers' influence on the Lucayan Islands and the region during the Americas' early colonization.

---

[1] The Taino people were indigenous inhabitants of nearby Hispaniola. The Lucayans and the Tainos are believed to be descendants of the same ethnic group that settled Hispaniola.

14

Historical Highlight

Names Previously Applied to The Bahamas & Turks and Caicos Islands

The Bahamas and Turks and Caicos Islands have shared at least one sub-regional name and four regional names as a single island chain over the past five centuries. The sub-regional name was Las Islas de Los Lucayos.[23] This name was exclusive to The Bahamas and Turks and Caicos Islands.

Las Islas de Los Lucayos means "Islands of the Lucayans" or "the Lucayan Islands."[24] Today, The Bahamas and the Turks and Caicos Islands are collectively called the Lucayan Islands or the Lucayan Archipelago. Spanish cartographers appended Las Islas de Los Lucayos (or Lucayas) to this stretch of islands sometime during the early 1500s.[25] In 1513, Spanish Conquistador Ponce de León described Grand Turk as part of the "Lucayos" during his expedition to Florida.[26]

The four regional names given to the island chain (as part of a wider geographic region) were: "Islands and the Mainland of the Indies in the Ocean Sea,"[27] the Antilles, the Spanish Main,[28] and the West Indies.

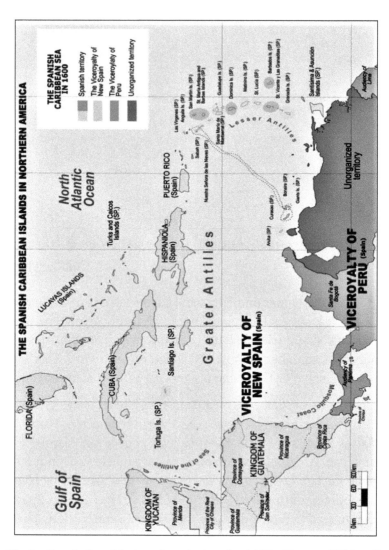

Illustration 4: Spanish Americas during the 1600s (Source: Wikimedia by Giggette)

The Spanish initially identified The Bahamas and Turks and Caicos Islands as "Islands" belonging to the "Mainland." The Spanish called this region "Islands and Mainland of the Indies in the Ocean Sea.[29] This misapplication is attributed to Columbus' mistaken belief that he had arrived in the Indies during his maiden transatlantic voyage. The Italian navigator thought he had reached the East Indies after making his first landfall in the Ancient World of the Western Hemisphere (now the Americas) in 1492.[30] However, Columbus had fallen short of the Indies by about 9,000 miles (14,484 Km).[31]

The Spanish mistakenly dubbed the Ancient World of the Western Hemisphere as "Islas y Tierra Firme." "Islas" (meaning "Islands") referred to the islands lying off East Asia's mainland, including Japan and the islands around Southeast Asia. "Tierra Firme" (meaning "Mainland") was the Spanish name for the Asian mainland.

The "Mainland" that the Spanish later explored in the Americas covered an area extending westward from Paria on Venezuela's north coast to Central America's east coast in the western Caribbean region. Paria's east coast is near Trinidad and Tobago in the southeastern Caribbean.[32] The "Islas" were the islands within the Caribbean region.[33]

According to maps used by Columbus, Europeans were unaware of the American continents. As far as the Europeans were concerned, the Ocean Sea was a vast maritime space between the Eastern and Western Hemispheres. Consequently, the Lucayan and Caribbean Islands were initially thought to be the "Islands in the Ocean Sea" off the Asian mainland.[34] [2]

---

[2] The waters encompassing the globe were once called The Ocean Sea before they were divided into oceans (for example, the Atlantic and Indian Oceans). Columbus was subsequently given the title Admiral of the Ocean Sea. See: Johnson, Lyman L., and Lipsett-Rivera, Sonya. (eds). (1998). The Faces of Honor: Sex, Shame, and Violence in

This erroneous belief lasted from 1492 until 1501 when Amerigo Vespucci realized that the islands and mainland Columbus happened upon belonged to a world previously unknown to Spanish explorers.[35] "Antilles" is another name ascribed to the islands within the Caribbean region, including the Lucayan Islands. The name Antilles was derived from a mythical island believed to be in the Atlantic Ocean west of Portugal [36] Today, the northern Caribbean Islands (including Cuba, Hispaniola (the Dominican Republic and Haiti), Puerto Rico, Jamaica, and the Cayman Islands) are called the Greater Antilles. The remaining Islands forming the north-south arc in the eastern Caribbean are called the Lesser Antilles.

The name Spanish Main was the third regional name to include The Bahamas and Turks and Caicos Islands. This name was the English version of the Spanish name Islas y Terra Firme.[37] The Spanish Main generally included the islands, coastal mainland areas, and waters within the Caribbean region. The fourth regional name to identify these islands is the "West Indies." The name West Indies (or the British West Indies) is still used to describe The Bahamas' and Turks and Caicos Islands' geographical location.

The term West Indies is also used to identify islands and territories within the Caribbean region that were former European colonies or are currently under the political jurisdiction of European countries, such as the Dutch West Indies and the French West Indies.

In addition to their archipelagic and regional names, The Bahamas and the Turks and Caicos Islands have had several name changes as politically separated territories. The Bahamas has had at least three name changes, and the Turks and Caicos Islands has had at least two.

Colonial Latin America. New Mexico: University of New Mexico Press. p.23.

The Turks and Caicos Islands were initially identified as two separate island groups after Bermudans began visiting them during the late 1670s. These groups were the Turks group and the Caicos group. In 1848, the two groups were collectively called the Turks and Caicos Islands.[38]

As for The Bahamas, the first name given to these islands as a separate entity was the "Bahama Islands." One of the earliest records of the Bahama Island chain being referred to as the Bahama Islands is found in the articles and orders for settling these islands by the Eleutheran Adventurers. The articles and orders were "made and agreed upon the 9th day of July, 1647"[39] to establish "the Plantation of the Islands of Eleutheria." These islands were "formerly called Buhama [Bahama] in America and the adjacent islands ...."[40]

In 1670, English authorities included the names "Bahama Islands" and "Lucayos" in a grant to six Lords Proprietors by the British Crown at the beginning of the proprietary government period for these islands. These Lords Proprietors took over the management of the Bahama Colony from the Eleutheran Adventurers. This grant included the "Bahama Islands . . . and all other islands lying within 22 degrees to 27 degrees commonly called the Bahama Islands or the Lucayos."[41] However, the area covered in the 1670 grant excluded the Turks and Caicos Islands.

The name Bahama Islands (as related to the Bahama archipelago) became a permanent fixture after the British Crown ended the proprietary government system and took direct control of the Bahama Islands in 1718. The change from proprietary to Crown governance occurred after Woodes Rogers was appointed the Bahama Colony's first Royal Governor. Rogers was commissioned as "Captain General and Governor in Chief in and over our Bahama Islands in America given at our court of Saint James the 6th day of February 1718, in the fourth year of our reign."[42]

The name Bahama Islands was also mentioned in the "The Bahama Islands (constitution) Order in Council 1963"[43] and was formally used until 1969. Consequently, the British Crown identified the Lucayan Islands as the Bahama Islands throughout the Eleutheran Adventurers (1648 to 1670), proprietary government (1670 to 1718), and Crown colony (1718 – 1973) periods.

Of note is that colonial authorities used the name "Bahamas" as an abbreviated form of the name Bahama Islands (or the plural form of the word Bahama). The abbreviated version of the Bahama Islands was evidenced in official correspondence (dated 1779) between the Bahama Colony and Great Britain. In the 1779 correspondence, the colonial authorities used "Bahamas" instead of Bahama Islands.[44] Examples of single name usage to collectively represent continents, regions, or islands within a hemisphere are titles such as the Americas, the West Indies, and the Exumas.

The second name applied to the Bahama Archipelago was "The Commonwealth of The Bahama Islands." This name was adopted in 1969, four years before the Bahama Colony was granted independence.[45] The third and current name for the Bahama Islands is "The Commonwealth of The Bahamas." The Bahamas Government agreed upon this name upon gaining independence on 10 July 1973.

Overall, The Bahamas and the Turks and Caicos Islands share one sub-regional name and four regional names. Additionally, The Bahamas has had at least three name changes, and the Turks and Caicos Islands has had two before the two countries were given their current names after being politically separated.

Chapter 3

The Name "Bahama"—Lucayan or Spanish?

For many years, the popular view has been that the name "Bahamas" originated from the Spanish word "bajamar" (or baja mar), meaning "low tide."[46] Coincidentally, the Spanish pronunciation of the word bajama (meaning shallow sea) is similar to the English pronunciation of the name Bahama. In the minds of many Bahamians and some scholars, the name Bahama means "shallow water"[47] or "shallow sea."[48] Understandably, the Spanish meaning of this name is descriptive of The Bahamas' reef-filled, shallow waters. However, this book proposes six reasons why Bahama is an indigenous name and not of Spanish origin.

The early evidence of the name Bahama being of Taino origin is found in Julian Granberry's and Gary Vescelius' research.[49] These scholars posit that Bahama comes from the Taino word "Bahama," which means "large upper middle land." Interestingly, each inhabited Lucayan Island had a Taino-derived name at the time of European contact.

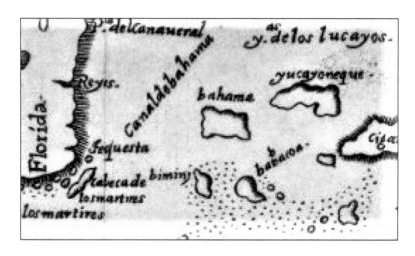

Illustration 5: A dissection of Antonio de Herrera y Tordesillas'1601 map displaying Grand Bahama as Bahama Island and the Straits of Florida as Canal de Bahama (Bahama Channel) in his book titled Historia general de los hechos de los castellanos en las Islas i Tierra Firme del Mar Oceano (General history of the events of the Castilians in the Islands and Tierra Firme of the Ocean Sea). (Courtesy: Library of Congress).

Granberry was the Language Coordinator for Native American Language Services in Florida at the time of the research. Vescelius (deceased in 1962) was an archaeologist. The results of their study took the form of essays that Granberry published in the 2004 book *Languages of the Pre-Columbian Antilles.* [50]

The Taino language evolved from the Arawakan language spoken by tribes from South America. It is believed that the Arawaks who lived near the Orinoco River in northern Venezuela island-hopped their way in dug-out canoes from South America through the Caribbean Islands. These island Arawaks settled in the northern Caribbean Islands of Puerto Rico, Hispaniola, and Cuba, where they developed a distinct culture from South American (mainland) Arawaks that historians call Taino.

22

Illustration 6: Arawak Indian village in South America by G.W.C. Voorduin-Geheugen van Nederland (1860). (Source: Wikipedia)

In the Taino language, the toponymic morphemes for the name "Bahama" are "ba-," "ha-," and "ma-." (Toponymic morphemes are place names broken down into their smallest word units). "Ba-" means "big, great, and large," "ha-" means "upper, north(ern)," and "ma-" means "middle."[51] The name "Bahama" means "Large Upper Middle Land," or more precisely, "Large Upper Northern Land."[52]

The name "Bahama" was displayed on Spanish maps to identify a specific Lucayan Island in the northwest Bahamas. Bahama Island has been displayed and named on Spanish maps from as early as 1523[53] (or earlier). The word "Grand" was later added to during the European colonization of the Americas, changing the name to Grand Bahama Island. This addition was a natural fit, with Grand Bahama being the third-largest Bahamian island behind Andros and Inagua Islands.

In addition to Granberry's and Vescelius' research, the spelling of the name Bahama on Antonio de Herrera y Tordesillas' 1601 map (and other antique maps) provides a second reason that the name "Bahama" is of Lucayan and not Spanish origin. (See Illustration 5). The Lucayan Islands were collectively called "Y[as] de los Lucayos" on Antonio de Herrera y Tordesillas' map (Y[as] is an abbreviation of Yslas, old Spanish for "isles").[54]

Antonio's 1601 map specifically identified today's Grand Bahama Island as Bahama Island, which was spelled with the letter "h" and not a "j" (as in "baja mar"). Another example of the "h" used in Spanish names is found on the first European world map to include the Americas. This map was published on Juan de La Cosa's Universal Chart (Carta Universal, or world map) in 1500, a century before Antonio's map. On this map, the indigenous islands named Guanahani, which Columbus renamed San Salvador, and Habacoa were also spelled with the letter "h." These spellings further support the idea that the name Bahama was an indigenous name, as explained in the following paragraphs. [55]

Illustration 7: An artist's rendition of Christopher Columbus' landfall on San Salvador by John Vanderlyn

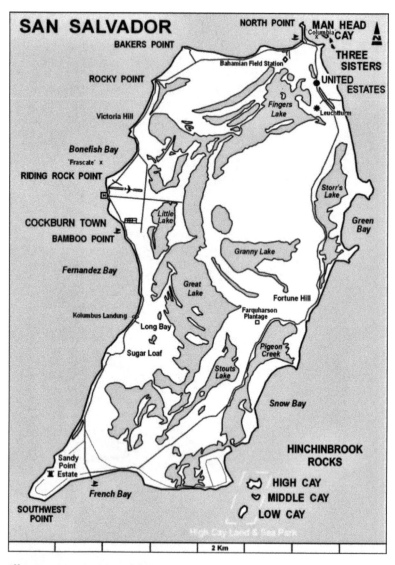

Illustration 8: Map of San Salvador Island, Bahamas. (Source: Wikipedia by Jamaicajoe)

Antonio's and Juan de La Cosa's maps provide early evidence that the spelling and usage of the name Bahama were not of Spanish origin but was an indigenous name for an individual island. Perhaps this was why cartographers initially applied the

26

name Los Lucayos and not Bahama to represent the entire chain of islands. Additionally, when Spanish orthography (conventional spelling system) is taken into consideration, it is farfetched to conceive that the name "Bahama" was derived from a corruption of the Spanish words "bajamar" or "baja mar" during the 1500s.

At that time, Spanish authorities did not interchangeably use the letter "j" with the letter "h."[56] If this were the case, then the name "Bahama" would have probably been spelled "baja mar" or "bajamar" (or "Baxamar"—an archaism at most) as in the name Baja California and not "Baha California.[57] Baha, California in northwest Mexico, was explored by the Spanish as early as 1539 and permanently settled in 1697.[58]

Also, if the name Bahama were of Spanish origin (meaning shallow sea), then there would be some logic in naming the chain of islands "Bajamar." However, the association of this name with the Spanish language does not appear to be the case other than the letter "j" in Spanish began sounding like an "h" in English, resulting in similar pronunciations for both baja mar and Bahama.

The Spanish language is historically rooted in the Latin language. Latin was previously known as Latium and was spoken in Rome. This language became the predominant language after Rome became a republic.[59] The letter "h" was part of the Roman alphabet. However, this letter had virtually disappeared from use during the early history of Classical Latin and was replaced by the letters "f" or "g" by 43 AD.[60]

The use of the letter "h" later resurfaced in northeastern Spain during the Roman occupation of Cantabria on the Iberian Peninsula. After the 13th century, the usage of this letter had spread southward through Spain. By the end of the 15th century, the letter "h" had virtually replaced the letter "f" on the Iberian Peninsula.[61]

Up until the early 16th century, Spanish and Italian authorities were keenly interested in reviving the classical languages, including Greek and Latin. This revival occurred during the Renaissance period when the "h" sound in words was vocalized. Although the vocalizing of the "h" sound was generally lost during the mid-1600s, the letter "h" was kept for etymological or historical reasons. Therefore, Spanish officials would not have changed the spelling of bajamar to Bahama.

The usage of "h" to designate the origins of indigenous names displayed "h" as a letter in its own right (and not as a mere corruption of the 'j'). The *Diccionario* or *Dictionary of the Royal Spanish Academy* (1726) also reinforced the use of the letter "h" in the Spanish alphabet for historical and etymological reasons.[62]

As a result, the letter "h" helped Spanish authorities trace the origins, pronunciations, and meanings of indigenous words. Similarly, the letter "h" also helped Granberry and Vescelius discover the origins and meaning of the word "Bahama."

The name of the island Bahama also appears in Gonzalo Fernández de Oviedo's book titled *Historia general y natural de las Indias* (or *History of the Indies*). In his book, Gonzalo Fernández de Oviedo lists the names of the Lucayan Islands stating:

...que cada una tiene su propio nombre y son muchas: así como Guanahaní, Caicos, Jumeto, Yabaque, Mayaguana, Samana, Guanima, Yuma, Curateo, Ciguateo, Bahama (que es la mayor de todas), el Yucayo y Necua, Habacoa e otras muchas isletas pequeñas que por allí hay.[63]

...that each has its own name, and they are many: such as Guanahani, Caicos, Jumeto, Yabaque, Mayaguana, Samana, Guanima, Yuma, Curateo, Ciguateo, Bahama (the largest of them all), the Yucayo and Necua, Habacoa and many other little islands that exist there.

Oviedo's observations provide a third reason why the name "Bahama" might not have come from the Spanish words "baja mar." It is noted that the island of Jumeto (in the Ragged Island chain) was spelled with the letter "j." The writers of the period had listed the name "Bahama" alongside other names of Lucayan origin with "h" without further commentary. The absence of an explanation for the variation of usage of these letters implies that the letter "h" in Bahama was distinct in pronunciation from the letter "j" in Spanish during the early exploration years.

Fourthly, the island "Bahama" was described as "the largest of them all," which is a description that is very closely related to the original meaning of the word *Bahama* in the Taino-Lucayan language as "Large Upper Middle Land." All of this strongly indicates the Taino origin of the name.

A fifth consideration is that it is not logical to apply a name that is derived from the Spanish words "baja mar," meaning "low tide" or "shallow sea," to a landmass. This application might have been plausible if the landmass was covered by water during high tide, which is not the case with Grand Bahama Island. Additionally, numerous rocks and shoals around the country only appear at low tide; however, none of these were ever named "Bahama."

Since the early written Spanish language, the letter "h" has been used at the beginning of Spanish words that begin with the letter "u," such as "huevo," "hueso," and "huerfano." It is uncertain if the letter "h" was used to represent a particular sound or if it existed to distinguish between a vowel or consonant, or both.[64] However, in the case of Native American words, it is believed that the Spanish chroniclers spelled the native words according to how they sounded when spoken by the Native Americans.[65]

Hence, the original pronunciation of the name "Bahama" was distinctly different from the pronunciation of the word "bajamar" by early Spanish speakers from Spain. As time progressed, Spanish descendants living in the Americas began to develop a cultural variation of the Spanish accent, which changed the pronunciations of some words. For example, the letter "j" was initially pronounced with a much stronger "h" sound by Spanish speakers from Spain during the early years of colonization.

However, as time progressed, the Spanish-American speakers had developed linguistic differences from the official Spanish language spoken in Spain. Spanish-speaking settlers in the Americas eventually pronounced the letter "j" with a softer "h" sound. As a result, the letter "j" began sounding more like the letter "h" as it does today, and the name "Bahama" became somewhat similar in pronunciation to the words "baja mar."

The sound of the letter "h" (and not "j") was also vocalized when pronouncing Taino words such as "huracan" (hurricane) or "hamaca" (hammock). It is believed that the Tainos, from whom the Lucayans descended, would have pronounced the letter 'h' with a soft 'h' sound, as heard in the English pronunciation of the letter.[66] The use of "h" in these instances would have emphasized the distinction in sounds between "j" and "h." Again this difference confirms that the name Bahama was of an indigenous origin and not a corruption of the Spanish word bajamar.

A sixth reason why the name Bahama is of Lucayan origin is that if the "h" sound in "Bahama" had been a much stronger Spanish "j" sound, rather than the softer "h" sound, the letter "j" would have been used. This is evident in written works of the late 15th to 16th-century Spanish authors, where the "h" is explicitly used to represent the popular discourse of both Andalusian and Spanish-American speakers.

Furthermore, Spanish explorers would have pronounced the word "baja" with a more distinctive "h" sound than pronounced today. Consequently, the "h" would not have been necessary, as seen in the spelling of the name of the northwestern Mexican state of "Baja California."

On the flip side, a less likely reason that the name "Bahama" might be of Spanish origin is the use of hiatuses. A hiatus is a word where the letter "h" separates two strong vowels adjacent to each other. Strong vowels in the Spanish language are the letters "a," "e," and "o." Spanish authorities used hiatuses to adopt Arab words and their different vocalization systems in the Spanish language.[67] This language integration was due to a cultural mix among the Spanish and the Arabic speakers following Spain's reconquest of Spanish territory on the Iberian Peninsula. The conflict lasted almost 800 years and ended in 1492.

Syllables in hiatuses are almost entirely blended in pronunciation. Examples of hiatuses are found in Spanish words with Arabic roots such as" azahar" ("aha") and "alcohol" ("oho").[68] If the Spanish used hiatuses in Lucayan words, the original spelling for "Bahama" would have been "Baama." The letter "h" would have been inserted between the two strong vowels of the letter "a" to form the word "Bahama." The same would have been done for the name Guanahani, which would have been spelled "Guanaani," and later spelled "Guanahani" after the "h" was used to separate the vowels. However, it is unlikely that hiatuses were used in these names for reasons previously stated.

In summation, it can be concluded that the name Bahama is an indigenous word of Taino origin and not a corruption of the Spanish word bajamar given the following:

31

- the toponymic morphemes for the Taino word Bahama (meaning Large Upper Middle of Northern Land) match the geographical features and location of (Grand) Bahama Island;
- the letter "h" was reintroduced to the Spanish language after many years of disuse and used during the Spanish conquest of the Americas;
- the letters "j" and the letter "h" had distinct sounds in Spanish during early Spanish explorations of the Americas;
- the letters "j" and "h" were not used interchangeably in the early Spanish language;
- the Taino-Lucayan people used words with the "h" sound in them;
- the Spanish language authorities spelled words with the "h" sound for historical and etymological reasons;
- Spanish cartographers displayed the name Bahama on charts as early as 1500 (eight years after Columbus' arrival);
- the Taino-Lucayan people pronounced the letter "h" in the names "Bahama" (now Grand Bahama) and "Guanahani" (now San Salvador) with a soft "h" sound;
- Spanish authorities spelled native words according to how the Native Americans pronounced them with an 'h' sound.

These observations further strengthen Granberry's and Vescelius' conclusion that the name "Bahama" is an indigenous name that the Lucayans used for today's Grand Bahama Island and is not a Spanish name as some believe.

Nevertheless, the question remains: How did the name of a single island (Bahama Island) in the extreme northwest corner of a 700 mile (1,126 km)-archipelago become the name of an entire country?

Historical Highlight

The Pronunciation Theory

While the Old and New Bahama Channels and the Great and Little Bahama Banks might have derived their Bahama names from (Grand) Bahama Island, there is another unlikely reason why the name Bahama might have been of Spanish origin. That reason has to do with the similarity of pronunciations of the Lucayan word "Bahama" and the Spanish words "baja mar," and how the meaning of these Spanish words is more relevant to the Bahama Islands than the meaning of the Lucayan word. For some, the name "Bahama" means "shallow sea." In Spanish, the words for "low tide" or "shallow sea" is "baja mar." These islands possess some of the largest shallow-water banks with the highest concentration of coral reefs in the region. The meaning of the Spanish words "baja mar" is more closely related to these islands' waters than the meaning of the name indigenous Taino-Lucayan name Bahama.

On the other hand, the Lucayan word Bahama means Large Upper Middle Land or Large Upper Northern Land.[69] As stated earlier, Bahama is the name of the Lucayan Island, now identified as Grand Bahama. This island is one of the Lucayan chain's largest islands.

Photo 3: Shallow water reef (Source: Wikipedia).

The belief that Bahama is of Spanish origin is perhaps due to the pronunciation of the words Bahama and baja mar are somewhat similar in sound. Additionally, the understanding that the Spanish definition (low tide or shallow sea) is more descriptive of the Lucayan waters and relevant to European mariners' hazardous experiences might have strengthened the belief among some historians and Bahamians that the word Bahama is of Spanish origin.

If this were the case, some confusion might have occurred between the Lucayan name (Bahama) and the Spanish pronunciation of the word bajamar. The meaning of this Spanish word (shallow sea) could have further reinforced the belief that the Lucayan name was of Spanish origin.

Regardless of the Bahama name's historical roots, it would be safe to say that what exists today is a country whose name is Lucayan in origin but carries a Spanish meaning (shallow sea) in the minds of some.

Chapter 4

Lucayan Island Names on Maps

Name changes on European maps relevant to the Ancient World of the Western Hemisphere began in the late 1400s with the arrival of European explorers. The Lucayan Islands were first claimed by Spain in 1492 and were among the first to be renamed by Columbus upon making landfall in this ancient world. Navigators typically chart new territories for future references. Though there is no record of it, the Lucayan Islands would have naturally been the first to be sketched on a map representing the Americas by Columbus (or Juan de la Cosa) during their first voyage to the Americas. This map would have come in handy during Columbus' second voyage to the Americas in 1493.

Juan de La Cosa had accompanied Columbus on his first voyage to the Americas and was the only map maker to give a firsthand account of the Lucayan Islands from a cartographer's perspective. Although Columbus never returned to the Lucayan Islands after departing them in 1492, historical records indicate that the Spanish were actively engaged in slave raiding in these islands from as early as 1499.[70] The raids continued until the islands were left depleted of their native inhabitants sometime between 1520[71] and 1530.[72]

Spanish interest shifted away from the Lucayan Islands after being stripped of their indigenous population. Though the Spanish never formally relinquished the Lucayan Islands until 1783, the Lucayan Islands were "up for grabs" by European powers by the mid-1500s. The English were the first to claim the Bahama Islands in 1629. However, English authorities made no effort to colonize them until 1648, after the English Crown granted the Eleutheran Adventurers a charter to settle the islands. Nevertheless, the Spanish names for the archipelago and a number of the original Lucayan Islands remained on maps throughout the Spanish colonial era from the 1500s to the early 1800s

The Lucayans had given each island a name.[73] Name changes began when Columbus renamed six Lucayan Islands he saw while sailing southward towards Cuba from Guanahani Island during his first voyage. Guanahani was the first island Columbus renamed, calling it San Salvador.

Indigenous island names that were changed by other navigators and cartographers include: "Nema" (New Providence), "Korateo" or "warateto" (Exuma), "Yuma" (Long Island), "Habakowa" (Andros), "Sibateo" or "Ciguateo" in Spanish (Eleuthera), "Lukayaneke" or "Lucayoneque" (Abaco), "Abawana" (Grand Turk), and "Yukanaka" (Providenciales).[74] The names Bahama, Bimini, Samana, Inagua, and Mayaguana are Lucayan (or Lucayan-derived) names that remain in use today. (See Book 1, The Lucayan Islands for more details).

Unlike the Lucayans, European cartographers traditionally placed names of archipelagos such as the Lucayan Islands or Greater Antilles (northern Caribbean) and regions such as the West Indies or East Indies on maps under a single name. The name "Las Islas de Los Lucayos"[75] or "Las Lucayas"[76] was probably the first name given to the Lucayan chain of islands by the Spanish during the early 1500s.[77]

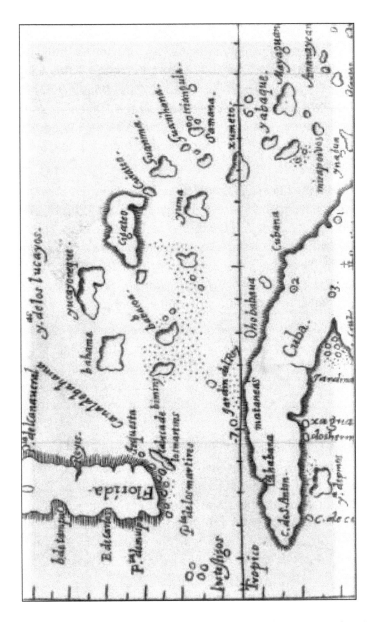

*Illustration 9: Antonio de Herrera y Tordesillas' 1601 map showing the
Lucayan Islands Yᵃˢ de los Lucayos (Source: Library of Congress)*

During the 1500s and 1600s, the name Lucayos appeared on maps in various European forms. As previously indicated, Spanish Conquistador Ponce de León referred to Turks Island as part of the "Lucayos" in 1513.[78] The Dominican Friar Bartolomé de Las Casas, also known as the "Defender of the Indians," documented the name Los Lucayos in his book *La Historia de las Indias*[79] (or *History of the Indies*), published in 1552.

From 1648, the Lucayan Islands were entirely under England's control except for the Spanish occupation from 1782 to 1783. Sometime around the 1700s, the name Bahama Islands began appearing more frequently on maps, along with Lucayos or Lucayas.[80] This dual naming (Lucayo or Bahama) of the Lucayan Archipelago continued through the 19th century, some 300 years after the Lucayan extinction.

For example, the *1818 Pinkerton Map of the West Indies, Antilles, and the Caribbean Sea* used "Lucayos or Bahama Islands" to represent the Lucayan Islands.[81] On this map, the names appear to refer to the Turks and Caicos Islands, which would have been under the Bahama Colony's administration when this map was published.

Some maps, such as the A.J. Johnson and Ward's 1864 map of "Cuba, Jamaica, and Porto Rico," displayed the name Bahama Islands without the name Lucayos during the latter half of the 19th century. Nonetheless, the name Lucayos (in reference to the Lucayan Archipelago) remained in use on maps for over three centuries before being entirely replaced by the name Bahama.

Historical Highlights

Examples of Island Name Changes on Maps

J uan de la Cosa was a navigator, cartographer, and the owner of Columbus' flagship, the Santa Maria. The world map he produced in 1500 was one of the first European world maps to include the Americas. This map was created approximately eight years after Columbus' historic trip. However, the exact geographic locations of the Lucayan Islands, such as San Salvador and Samana Cay, are unclear on the map.

Additionally, the 1523 Turin map of the Americas displays several Lucayan Islands with their Taino names.[82] On this map, Guanahani (the island of Columbus' first landfall) is shown where today's San Salvador Island is located.

The 1650 map by Dutch mapmaker Joan Vinckeboons titled "Map of a Part of the Island of Cuba and of the Bahamas" also shows San Salvador in the exact location on the 1523 Turin map.[83] Additionally, Vinckeboons' map features a number of the islands using their indigenous names. Grand Bahama is displayed as "Bahama," Cat Island as "Guanima," Eleuthera as "Ciguateo," and the Florida Straits as "Canael van Bahama" (the Bahama Canal).[84]

Illustration 10: A dissection of Spanish Cartographer and navigator Juan de la Cosa's 1500 world map showing Guanahani and its neighboring Lucayan Islands, including Samana Cay. (Source: Wikimedia)

As years passed, European maps displayed additional name changes among Lucayan Islands. A list of Lucayan and Spanish names for the Lucayan Islands is published in Book 2 (The Lucayan Islands). Waterways and cays with Spanish (or Spanish derived) names include: Straits of Florida, Mira Por Vos Passage (meaning He/She Watches over Us Passage), located south of Acklins Island in the southeastern Bahamas; and Cay Santo Domingo (Holy Sunday Cay) on the Great Bahama Bank's southern edge.

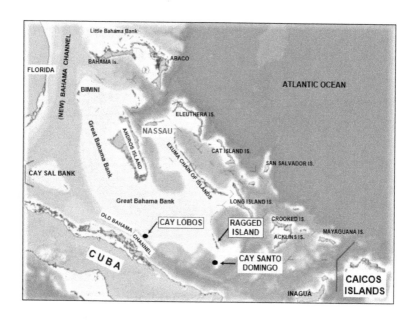

Illustration 11: Map displaying Cay Santo Domingo and Cay Lobos (Source: Wikimedia. Names inserted)

Cay Santo Domingo is a tiny remote cay just north of the area where four young Royal Bahamas Defence Force Marines lost their lives due to a Cuban jetfighter attack. Their 103-foot (31 meters) patrol craft, Her Majesty's Bahamian Ship (HMBS) Flamingo, sank near Cay Santo Domingo on 10 May 1980, the eve of Mother's Day Sunday. Fifteen officers and marines survived the incident.

The sinking of HMBS Flamingo was the first act of external aggression experienced by the newly independent Bahamas. About 123 miles (198 km) west of Santo Domingo is another isolated Bahamian cay on the Old Bahama Channel's northern side named Cay Lobos. This cay is about 15 miles (24 km) north of central Cuba on the north side of the Old Bahama Channel.

Photo 4: Her Majesty's Bahamian Ship (HMBS) Flamingo's original crewmembers. (Courtesy: Royal Bahamas Defence Force).

The Spanish name for the tiny cay was Cayo de Lobos (Cay of Wolves), named after the howling sounds of Caribbean Monk seals (now extinct) that once lived on the remote cay in the southern Bahama chain.[85] One of the larger and most populated islands in the Turks and Caicos Islands also has a Spanish name. Providenciales (or Providence in English) is located at the western end of the Caicos Island group, north of Haiti.

The 1805 map titled "*To his excellency Thos. Jefferson, esqr., president of the Congress, this chart of the United States of America: including Halifax, Havannah [Havana], New Providence, and all the northern parts of the West Indies*"[86] displays The Bahama Islands with Grand Bahama as Great Bahama, Abaco as Lucaya, the Exuma Sound as Rock Sound, San Salvador as Watland Island, and Cat Island as Guanahani.

Published in 1805 in London, this map also features the Tongue of the Ocean as the Gulf of Providence, Abaco as Lucaya, Little Inagua as Heneaga, Cay Lobos in the southern Bahamas as Cayo Lobos (Cay of Wolves), and the Caicos Islands as Caycos.[87] This map might have inspired the developers of Freeport in Grand Bahama to name their enclave Freeport-Lucaya).

The 1764 French map of the northern Bahamas titled "*Carte Des Isles Lucayes*" (Chart of the Lucayan Islands) shows Grand Bahama as "Ifle de Bahama" (meaning Isle of Bahama or Bahama Isle), the Florida Straits as "Canal de Bahama" (Bahama Canal), the Great Bahama Bank as "Pracel ou Le Banco ("Submerged Reef of the Bank"), and the Exuma Sound as Baye d'Exuma (Bay of Exuma).[88]

Some maps displayed the Florida Straits as the Bahama Channel, such as the 1776 map titled "*The coast of West F[lorid]a and Louisiana. The Peninsula and Gulf of Florida or Channel of Bahama with the [Bah]ama I[s]lands.*" This map was published in London during the year the United States' 13 colonies declared independence.[89]

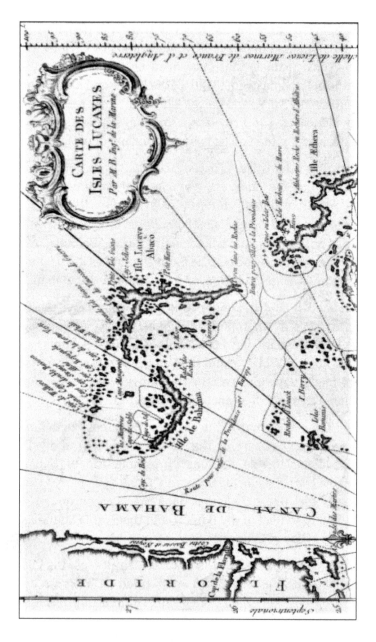

Illustration 12: A dissection of the 1764 French map Carte Des Lucayes. (Source: Library of Congress)

44

The 1782 Spanish map features the map of The Bahamas as *"Carta reducida de las islas Lucayas, ò de los Lucayos,"* meaning "The reduced chart of the Islands of the Lucayans [in its feminine form] or the Lucayans [in its masculine form]."[90] The map shows the Little Bahama Bank as Pequeño Banco de Bahama (meaning the Little Bank of Bahama) and Grand Bahama as Isla Grande de Bahama (the Grand Island of Bahama), indicating a direct connection between the Little Bahama Bank and Grand Bahama Island. It also displays the Great Bahama Bank as El Banco de Grande de Bahama (or the Grand Bank of Bahama).

Also displayed on this 1782 map is Great Abaco Island as "Lucayoneque or Abaco," the Exuma Sound as Bahia de Exuma (Bay of Exuma), Andros Island as "Islas Del Espiritu Santo de San Andres, ó Andros Islands" (meaning Islands of the Holy Spirit of Saint Andrew or Andros Island), Northwest Providence Channel as "Camino para venir de la Providencia á Europa" (Route to come from Providence to Europe), revealing an alternative passage from the Americas to Europe through The Bahamas' Northwest Providence Channel. Juan López had published this map in Madrid, Spain.[91]

New names or variations of these names were given to the islands by European authorities who took possession of them. The Spanish and the British were responsible for changing some of the indigenous names given to the Lucayan Islands.

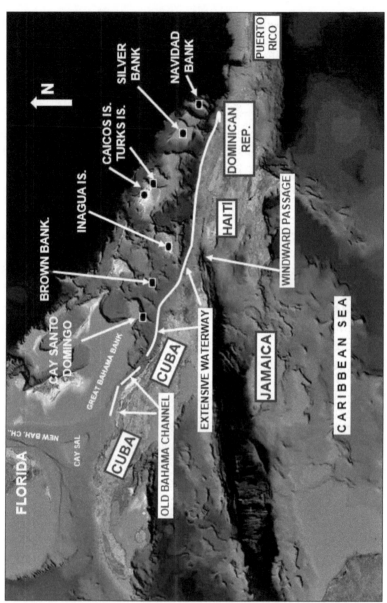

Illustration 13: Map of the Northern Caribbean showing Old Bahama Channel and the Extensive Waterway east of the Old Bahama Channel. (Source: Wikimedia. Names inserted. Not to scale).

Chapter 5

Discovery of the Old Bahama Channel

Columbus soon lost interest in the Lucayan Islands shortly after making landfall on the island of Guanahani (now San Salvador) in 1492. Columbus spent 14 days exploring the southern Lucayan Islands before his departure. Columbus did not find the gold or spices he sought. The friendly Lucayans welcomed Columbus to their shores and told him that gold could be found on the big island further south. Columbus departed the Lucayan Islands, becoming the first European to cross the channel (the Old Bahama Channel) separating the Lucayan Islands from the Caribbean Islands.

The channel is located between the north coast of central Cuba and the southern boundary of the Great Bahama Bank. The channel's strategic location gave European ships access to the Americas and allowed outbound vessels to return to Europe through the North Atlantic Ocean. The Old Bahama Channel's western end is about 130 miles (210 km) south of the New Bahama Channel.

The Old Bahama Channel generally runs in a northwest-southeast direction for about 100 miles (160 km) along central Cuba's north coast in the area of the Sabane-Camaguey Archipelago. The channel is about 15 miles (24 km) wide at its narrowest point near the center, gradually widening towards its eastern and western ends. The channel's western end is about 250 miles (400 km) east of Cuba's capital city, Havana, and Havana's Harbor. The Old Channel is fringed with rocks, shoals, and cays on both sides.

After exploring the central Cuban coast, Columbus exited the eastern end of the Old Bahama Channel and entered the extensive (unnamed) waterway adjoining it. After entering this waterway, he continued his eastbound journey. This waterway is much wider than the Old Bahama Channel and is approximately 600 miles (570 km) long.

One of the widest areas along the waterway lies between Cay Santo Domingo (approximately 34 miles/55 km south of the Ragged Island chain in The Bahamas) and Guardalavaca town (near Cuba's southeastern end). Cay Santo Domingo is on the channel's northern edge, and Guardalavaca is on its southern boundary. The distance between the two landmarks is about 40 miles (65 km).

On the northern side of the waterway are the southern borders of The Bahamas, including Great Bahama Bank, the Ragged Island chain (Cay Santo Domingo), Brown Bank (midway between Ragged Island and Great Inagua), and Great Inagua Island. Also on the northern side of the waterway are the southern borders of the Turks and Caicos Islands, the Mouchoir Bank, the Silver Bank, and the La Navidad Bank, with deepwater between the islands and the banks. On the waterway's southern side are Cuba's Guantanamo province at the southeastern end of the island, the Windward Passage's northern end, and the north coast of Hispaniola (Haiti and the Dominican Republic).

At the eastern entrance of this waterway is the Samana Peninsula (on the Dominican Republic's northeast coast) and the La Navidad Bank, about 70 miles (112 km) north of the Peninsula. La Navidad Bank is a reef that is awash in some areas and is located approximately 180 miles (290 km) southeast of

Grand Turk. This bank is also a geological part of the Lucayan Island chain located at the chain's southeastern end. However, the bank falls under the Dominican Republic's territorial jurisdiction.

The Old Bahama Channel's extensive waterway's geographical layout makes it an unconventional channel. (This writer refers to this unnamed waterway as *the Old Bahama Channel Extensive Waterway* for this book's purposes). Spanish ships exiting the eastern end of the Old Bahama Channel en route to Spain from Havana sailed an additional 600 miles (1,000 km) of potential maritime hazards along the waterway, albeit in a wider maritime space than the Bahama Channel.

Apart from threats of pirates, privateers, and enemy warships, Spanish treasure ships and fleets became channel-locked when caught in hurricanes in this southern channel. The threat of storms spelled double doom (structural damages and groundings) for the unfortunate vessels. Ships suffered irreparable damage as violent winds and waves tossed them onto unforgiving reefs bordering the channel.

After exiting the Old Bahama Channel Extensive Waterway, Columbus arrived off the northwest coast of Hispaniola, where he attempted to establish the Americas' first European settlement on Haiti's northeast coast. The settlement was named La Navidad and consisted of a makeshift fort constructed from materials salvaged from his flagship, the Santa Maria. The Santa Maria had grounded off Haiti's northeast coast on Christmas Eve in 1492. Thirty-nine of Columbus' men were left behind to guard the fort and search for gold until Columbus returned.

After departing Haiti, Columbus made his way toward the east end of the extensive waterway. His last stop in the Ancient World of the Western Hemisphere was near the Samaná Peninsula on the northeast coast of the Dominican Republic in January 1493. After departing Hispaniola, Columbus headed northeastward to cross the Atlantic Ocean, completing his first voyage to the Americas on 15 March 1493.

That same year, Columbus returned to the Americas as Governor of Hispaniola, where he learned that the Tainos massacred all of the men he had left behind at La Navidad. Columbus later founded La Isabela (1493 – 1496/1497).[92] La Isabela was located on the northwest coast of the Dominican Republic, not far from the Haitian border. Santo Domingo was the last settlement established under Columbus' governorship. The town was founded on the Dominican Republic's southwest coast in 1496. (See Book 2 for details).

Altogether, Columbus made four trips to the Americas. During his first trip, he navigated parts of the Old Bahama Channel and the Extensive Waterway adjoining it. He also sailed through a portion of the Extensive Waterway back to Spain during his second voyage. However, he did not use the Old Bahama Channel or the Extensive Waterway during his third and fourth trips to the New World.

After Hispaniola's colonization began, the Spanish launched a series of expeditions throughout the northern Caribbean. In 1511, Conquistador Diego Velázquez de Cuéllar began his conquest of Cuba. Spanish ships made greater use of the old channel as more trips to Cuba were carried out, and Spanish settlements in Cuba increased. Velázquez became Cuba's first Governor and founded the township of Baracoa at the southeastern end of Cuba's northern coast in 1512. The town's northern limits faced the extensive waterway east of the Old Bahama Channel.

Havana's first settlement (or Old Town) was founded in 1519, with the town being designated "Llave del Nuevo Mundo y Antemural de las Indias Occidentales" ("Key to the New World and Rampart of the West Indies") by a royal decree. The decree highlighted the town's significance in exploiting the "Indies" wealth. Havana subsequently became a strategic base of operations for Spanish ships and convoys returning from or returning to Spain. In 1553, the Governor's residence was moved to Havana, making Havana the capital of Cuba.[93]

Spanish authorities shipped gold to Spain from townships in the northern Caribbean islands of Santo Domingo (the Dominican Republic), Caparra (Puerto Rico), and Havana (Cuba). Before the new route to Spain was discovered and later named the Bahama (or New) Bahama Channel, ships returning to Spain generally followed Columbus' return route from the northern Caribbean. In 1519, a new passage was discovered further north. Although it was considered a faster voyage to Spain due to the northward flow of the Gulf Steam, this new channel was equally treacherous as the old channel.

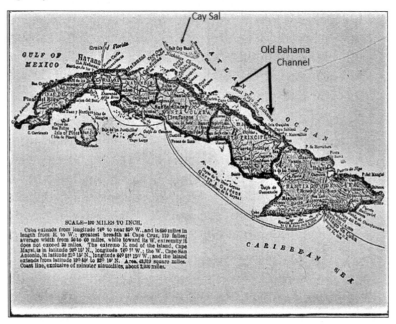

Illustration 14: 1899 map of Cuba showing the Old Bahama Channel as Canal Viejo de Bahama. (Source: Wikipedia).

Nonetheless, Spanish fleets continued using the old channel (later named the Old Bahama Channel) that ran along central

Cuba's north coast. This continuation may have been due to fear of the channel's strong currents, the enemy's presence, or a lack of navigational skills and confidence among ships' captains.

Ships belonging to fleets such as the 1691 Spanish plate (silver) fleet made it safely through the old channel.[94] However, others like the Spanish ship Nuestra Señora de la Pura y Limpia Concepción, were not as fortunate. The Nuestra Señora had taken the old channel route and ran aground on the Silver Bank after being caught in a hurricane in 1641. The Nuestra was laden with silver at the time of the incident at the eastern end of the extensive waterway,[95] giving the bank its name (Silver Bank).

One of the earliest Spanish wrecks in the Extensive Waterway is the Molasses Reef Wreck. This wreck also occurred near the eastern end of the waterway in1513 and is "the oldest European wreck excavated in the Western Hemisphere." Molasses Reef is about 20 miles (32 km) south of Providenciales, on the western edge of the Caicos Bank.[96]

Located between The Bahamas and Cuba, The Old Bahama Channel establishes the geographical limits between the Lucayan and Caribbean Islands. The channel is the oldest known channel discovered by European mariners in the Americas. However, mariners soon began using this new channel as news of its discovery broke. The usage of this channel had a significant impact on the Bahama Islands' name.

Today, the Old Bahama Channel is a main passageway for cruise ships and merchant vessels entering, departing, or transiting through the Americas. The Old Bahama Channel is now under the territorial jurisdictions of The Bahamas and Cuba, with its northern half belonging to The Bahamas and its southern half belonging to Cuba.

Chapter 6

Discovery of the New Bahama Channel

Spanish interests in the Caribbean Islands faded as new Spanish colonies grew on the more lucrative American mainland during the early 1500s. During this period, Spanish Conquistador Hernán Cortés' drew much attention to Mexico and the American continent as he engaged in conquering the gold-rich Aztec Empire. Other conquistadors such as Francisco de Montejo el Adelantado and Francisco Pizarro mounted their conquests of the Mayan and Inca Empires in Central and North America. These conquests took place when the Lucayan Islands were nearing total depopulation.

Memories of the Lucayans live on through the name the Spanish name gave the Lucayan Archipelago, Islas de Los Lucayos (or Lucayan Islands). With time, the name Bahama, which the Lucayans called today's Grand Bahama Island, was applied to the channel adjacent to the island by the Spanish. Perhaps the most telling reason for this name change was the discovery of a new return route to Spain in 1519 for Spanish vessels departing the Americas. This new route was a waterway off Grand Bahama Island's west coast. Ponce de León traversed this area from the northern Bahamas six years earlier during his

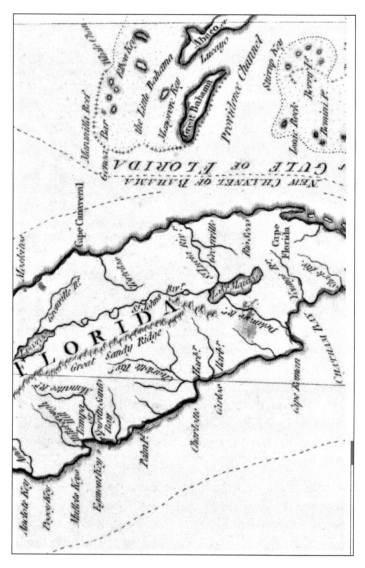

Illustration 15: Dissection of the 1781 map of "East and West Florida, Georgia, and Louisiana: with the islands of Cuba, Bahama, and the countries surrounding the Gulf of Mexico, with the tract of the Spanish galleons, and of our fleets thro' the Straits of Florida" by Bew, John, and Lodge, John. (Source: Library of Congress)

expedition to Florida in 1513, but he never fully explored it. Ponce de León's voyage took him along the entire eastern seaboard of the Lucayan chain to Florida from Puerto Rico. It was unknown, at the time, that this waterway was a channel that could be used for returning to Europe. However, in 1519, Anton de Alaminos, one of Conquistador Hernan Cortés' ships' captains, became the first mariner to navigate the channel's full length during a special assignment to Spain. Anton was pressed to explore the channel when Cortés was preparing for an all-out attack against the Aztecs in Mexico.

The Spanish navigator had first-hand experience navigating the New Bahama Channel and its strong northerly currents during Ponce de León's maiden voyage to Florida from Puerto Rico. Ponce de León became the first European to make landfall on the North American continent that would later become part of the United States.

Anton's maritime career began as a cabin boy aboard Columbus' ships during Columbus' fourth and final voyage to the Americas in 1502. Anton also took part in Spanish Conquistador Hernández de Córdoba's 1517 voyage to the Yucatan Peninsula, and Conquistador Juan de Grijalva's expedition to Mexico in 1518. [97] Moreover, Anton was acquainted with Cortés' plans to conquer the Aztecs.

In 1519, Hernán Cortés' hand-picked Anton for a special assignment to Spain. Cortés subsequently dispatched Anton with two of his (Cortés') alcaldes (or mayors), Francisco de Montejo and Alonso Hernández de Puerto Carrero, from Mexico. The Montejo and Hernández were mayors of a town Cortés founded on the southwest coast of Mexico's Atlantic coast. Cortés trusted Anton as a highly experienced pilot and relied on his noblemen to represent him before the Holy Roman Emperor, King Charles V of Spain (also known as King of Spain

Charles I). Both mayors were experienced in maritime affairs and given responsibility for the overall mission to Spain, thereby playing a critical role in its success at sea.

Earlier that year, Cuban Governor Diego Velázquez de Cuéllar deployed Cortés to explore the Mexican Atlantic coast but ordered Cortés to abort the expedition shortly after his deployment. Cortés' zealous ambitions overrode Velázquez' change of plans for Mexico. In defying Velázquez's orders, Cortés continued his voyage to Mexico, where he discovered an abundance of gold.

Illustration 16: Cortés and La Malinche (an enslaved indigenous interpreter) meet Moctezuma II, Emperor of Aztec Empire, in Tenochtitlán, November 8, 1519 (Source: Wikipedia)

Having laid eyes on Mexico's gold and realizing a rare opportunity to achieve greatness, Cortés sought the governorship of Mexico for himself. As a result, he founded Villa

Rica de la Vera Cruz (now Veracruz) on Mexico's southeastern coast. This move created an opportunity for Cortés to be elected Captain-General and Chief Justice of the new Spanish territory by his soldiers, who were considered citizens of the town. Cortés hoped that his self-appointment would free him from Velázquez's control and the consequences of defying Velázquez's orders.[98]

Cortés also hatched a plan behind Velázquez's back to seek the King of Spain's favor to appoint him Governor of Mexico. He subsequently dispatched Anton as captain of a vessel loaded with gold for the King, along with his envoys, to seal the deal.[99]

The treasure from Mexico was sent as a personal gift to persuade the King in Cortés' favor. The loot consisted of elaborate ornaments, including a gold and silver wheel and shields made with gold.[100] Before departing Mexico for Spain, Anton replenished supplies in Havana, Cuba. Anton initially intended to use the Old Bahama Channel route on Cuba's north coast to reach Spain.

However, news of his intentions was leaked before departing Cuba's harbor. Velázquez subsequently dispatched a vessel in the Old Bahama Channel to intercept Anton's ship as it headed east. After determining his escape options, Anton decided to outmaneuver the arresting craft by heading north toward the unexplored waterway.[101] During the episode, Montejo and Hernández supported Anton's crucial decision to make a run for the new channel to avoid capture by Cortés' Spanish rivals in Cuba. Anton navigated the full length of the new channel for the first time with the hope of making good his escape to Spain.

Spanish mariners were unfamiliar with the strong currents associated with the channel and the unforgiving reefs near Florida. Understandably, these mariners were doubtful if the waterway was passable and uncertain about its currents' impact on their ships.

Photo 5: Map showing western and central Grand Bahama Island. (Source: Wikipedia. Names inserted)

Nonetheless, Anton's past experiences, navigational skills, and courage led him to use the new channel. The alcaldes agreed with Anton's snap decision, and the men escaped their would-be captors. The mission was a total success for Cortés' envoys, who arrived safely in Spain. Spanish annals describe Anton as "the most experienced pilot of that sea."[102] Cortés later defeated the Aztecs and was appointed Governor of New Spain during the colonization of Mexico.[103]

Anton's successful passage through the channel confirmed that the waterway was a viable route to Spain. The channel was later named the Bahama Channel (or the New Bahama Channel) and became a primary route for Spanish treasure ships.

Chapter 7

Drama in the Bahama Channel

After the Bahama Channel (or New Bahama Channel) was discovered, Spanish ships traveled northward from Cuba through the new channel between Florida and The Bahamas. The Bahama Channel runs from south to north for ships departing Cuba. On the channel's west side is South Florida's east coast. (See Illustration 20).

At the edge of the channel's eastern boundary is the Bimini Island chain. This chain of islands is near the Bahama Channel's southern section and borders the Great Bahama Bank's western edge. The chain comprises North and South Bimini Islands at its northern end, with a string of islands stretching southwards to Orange Cay, about 57 miles (92 km) from North Bimini. North Bimini is roughly 57 miles (93 km) east of Miami, Florida.

Ocean Cay is in the middle of the chain, and its name was changed to Ocean Cay MSC Marine Reserve after the Mediterranean Shipping Company (MSC) purchased the manmade cay in 2015. The cay is approximately 66 miles (106 km) southeast of Miami and is now used as a cruise island for MSC. (See Illustration 20).

Also, on the channel's eastern side (near the Bahama Channel's mid-section) is the western end of the Northwest Providence

Channel. Additionally, (Grand) Bahama Island and the Little Bahama Bank are on this side of the Bahama Channel but at the Bahama Channel's northern end. Grand Bahama is about 66 miles (106 km) from Palm Beach on Florida's east coast. From the north end of the Little Bahama Bank (Matanilla Shoal) to Orange Cay is 167 miles (268 km).

Upon exiting the (New) Bahama Channel's northern end, ships' captains later altered course northeastward for Spain. This route allowed mariners to maximize the use of the northward flow of the Gulf (of Mexico's) current (or Gulf Stream) through the channel, as well as the easterly flow of the North Atlantic Ocean's gyre (circular current) in the ocean's northern sector, effectively shortening the duration of their voyages from Cuba.

Bahama Island was the last landmark that mariners saw on the eastern side of the channel as they exited the channel, depending on how close they were to the island. Mariners were required to maintain a vigilant lookout for Bahama Island, the Little Bahama Bank, and their fringing reefs whenever transiting the channel. Navigating the channel was detrimental during storms and hurricanes. The possibility of surprise pirate attacks on treasure ships sailing through the Bahama Channel added to the dread of Spanish mariners. Rival European powers' incursions by states such as England, France, and the Netherlands threatened Spanish dominance and economic interests in the Americas.

The founding of European enemy settlements on the Florida east coast posed a real and present danger to Spanish ships sailing through the adjacent Bahama Channel. Consequently, Spanish fortifications were needed around the Florida coast to protect or repair Spanish ships and provide refuge during storms. [104] In 1564, a Spanish expeditionary force under Spanish Conquistador Pedro Menéndez de Avilér destroyed a French (Huguenot) Fort in the area of Saint John's River (River of Mary) near modern-day Jacksonville on the Florida east coast. Many French colonists were slaughtered during the incident.

Following the conflict, the Spanish built their first permanent settlement in what is now part of the United States of America. The settlement was founded in 1565 near the old French Fort and was named Saint Augustine after the Catholic theologian Saint Augustine. Today, Saint Augustine is the oldest permanent European township in the United States.[105] In 1658, the French avenged the deaths of their Huguenot colonists with naval ships launching a surprise attack on the Spanish town of San Mateo, 30 miles (48 km) southwest of St. Augustine, Florida. Hundreds of Spaniards were killed, but the French never attempted to colonize Florida following the conflict.[106]

Just over a century after Spain began colonizing the North American mainland, the Eleutheran Adventurers from Bermuda resettled the Bahama Islands. Farming on these islands was unproductive. Many English colonists occupied themselves with shipwrecking (retrieving salvageable goods from sunken ships) and became known as "wreckers." Bahamian wreckers traveled as far west as the Florida Keys to practice their trade up until the early 1800s.[107] The Spanish were troubled by Bahamians trespassing their turf and salvaging their vessels in Bahamian and Florida waters.

The Golden Age of Piracy (roughly 1650 – 1730) in the Caribbean region also took shape during the Bahama Colony's founding. During the 1600s, Bahamians were scorned as "descendants of pirates and members of a lawless race."[108] The fraternization of proprietary governors with pirates in the Bahamas presented a serious threat to Spanish ships in the region. Even worse, the absence of governance between 1704 and 1718 created an opportunity for pirates to infest the islands. The administrative void allowed the maritime outlaws to boldly declare New Providence the Pirate Republic[109] from 1706 to 1718. [110]

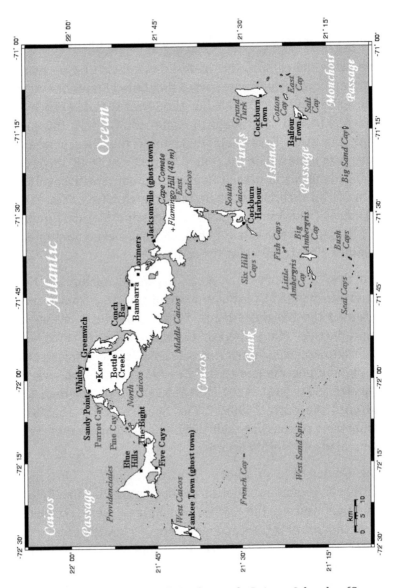

Illustration 17: Map of Turks and Caicos Islands. (Source: Wikipedia by Kelisi).

The presence of pirates and ship wreckers around the Turks and Caicos Islands exacerbated the tense Spanish-British relations. Spain and its European allies were also at war with England during the 1600s and 1700s. Shipwrecking, piracy, and rivalry between European powers were an explosive mix of activities for colonists in the Lucayan Islands. This combination was an open invitation for England's arch enemies to invade The Bahamas and Turks and Caicos Islands and burn their settlements. Spanish naval forces were based at Cuban ports with direct access to the Old Bahama Channel and were in striking distance of the Lucayan Islands. The Bahamas and the Turks and Caicos Islands experienced repeated attacks by Spanish and French forces during the 1600s and 1700s.

Spain later introduced annual naval escorts for its vessels in the Pacific and Atlantic Oceans to protect its ships. On the Atlantic side, two fleets, each comprising 60 to 90 Spanish ships, arrived in the Americas annually. [111] Surprisingly, most casualties suffered by Spanish vessels in the Americas was not due to pirate attacks or battles at sea with rival powers. Out of the estimated 681 Spanish ships lost from 1492 to 1898, about 91 percent of the Spanish fleet and thousands of lives were lost due to terrible storms and hurricanes, which aptly fit the Taino origin of the word hurricane (Huracán), meaning storm or evil spirit according to some sources.[112]

Approximately 1.4 percent of Spanish ships were lost from naval engagements, and 0.8 percent of total losses were due to pirate attacks.[113] Columbus' flagship, the Santa Maria, became the first Spanish ship lost in the Americas after running aground off Hispaniola's (Haiti's) north coast. The destroyer Plutón was the last Spanish ship that sank in the Americas after the US Navy destroyed it off Cuba's north coast during the Spanish-American War in 1898.

Also lost were tons of treasure on the Great and Little Bahama Banks. The incidents in, near, or around the Bahama Channel made the name "Bahama" famous (or more precisely infamous) among European explorers, cartographers, and authorities during the exploitation of the Americas' wealth.

The Old Bahama Channel was used for Spanish explorations, colonization, and exploitation as a primary navigation route. English, French, and Dutch pirates also used the channel. As territories in the region changed hands, the Old Bahama Channel became a crucial maritime artery for Britain to smuggle goods and supplies into U.S. ports from its Bahama Colony during the American Revolution (1775 – 1783). Following the U.S. declaration of Independence and Spain and England's decline in naval supremacy, conflicts within the Old Bahama Channel faded away. However, the channel is still used as a major intercontinental and intracontinental shipping waterway.

Chapter 8

How the Old and New Bahama Channels & Banks Got their Names

Despite the inherent dangers of the Bahama Channel, news of Anton de Alaminos' safe passage to Spain through the Bahama Channel made the newly discovered channel a strategic route for Spanish treasure ships returning to Spain. Ships sailing northbound from Havana, Cuba, traveled northward, passing Cay Sal Bank near the eastern entrance of the Gulf of Mexico before arriving at the Bahama Channel's southern end. Upon entering the channel, the vessels' speed accelerated due to the northerly current flowing out of the Gulf of Mexico, known as the Gulf Stream.

The strong current flows northward along the North American coast, eventually making its way eastward across the northern boundary of the Atlantic Ocean. Spanish ships departing Cuba followed the current's flow before heading east for Spain.

The ships' eastward voyage was assisted by the easterly flow of the North Atlantic Oceans' circulation (gyre), which further hastened their return voyage to Spain. The Little Bahama Bank is adjacent to the northern end of the New Bahama Channel and is about 5,500 square miles (14,200 sq. km.).[114]

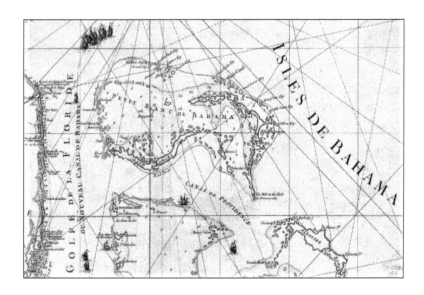

Illustration 18: A dissection of a 1771 French map by Georges-Louis Le Rouge and Thomas Jefferys displaying the Florida Straits as Golfe de La Florida ou Nouveau Canal de Bahama (or New Canal of Bahama) with a track line followed by ships through the channel (Source: US Library of Congress).

This bank is lined with dangerous shoals and shifting sand bars. At the southwest corner of this bank is (Grand) Bahama Island. Ponce de León and Anton de Alaminos learned of this island's indigenous name (Bahama) from other Spaniards who Ponce de León met off the coast of this island during his 1513 expedition.

Abaco Island occupies a larger portion of the Little Bahama Bank than (Grand) Bahama Island, and Florida is much larger than Bahama Island. Nonetheless, mariners and cartographers appear to have associated the channel and its neighboring bank more with Bahama Island than with Abaco Island or Florida and subsequently named the channel the Bahama (or New Bahama) Channel rather than calling it the Abaco or Florida Channel. Furthermore, Florida was not permanently colonized until the 1560s. Hence, the name Florida might not have generated much interest as a navigational point of reference when the Bahama Channel was named.

It is also noted that Anton became familiar with the island the Lucayans called Bahama during Ponce de León's voyage to Florida in 1513. It is further noted that Ponce de León's crossing of the channel adjacent to Bahama Island would have revealed that the channel's waterway provided access to the Atlantic Ocean at its northern end. During the same trip, both Ponce de León and Anton learned that the channel provided access to Cuba. The knowledge that this waterway connected Cuban waters with the Atlantic Ocean would have helped Anton in his split decision to use the channel as an escape route to Spain in 1519.

It is reasonable to believe that Anton included Bahama Island and its adjacent channel in his report to Spanish authorities upon his arrival in Spain in 1519. It also appears that Spanish mariners and cartographers associated Anton's new route with Bahama Island. Bahama Island's proximity to the adjacent bank and the newly discovered channel made the island's name (Bahama) a logical choice for naming the channel and bank next to it the Bahama Channel and the (Little) Bahama Bank.

An early reference to the Bahama Channel's name is found on Antonio de Herrera y Tordesillas' 1601 map. This map displays the channel's name as Canal de Bahama.[115] Interestingly, the Great Bahama Bank and the Old Bahama Channel at the southern end of the Bahama chain have geographical features and navigational hazards that closely resemble the Little Bahama Bank and the Bahama Channel features. (See Illustration 5).

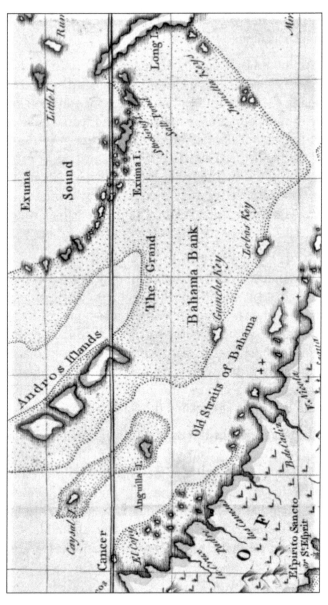

Illustration 19: A dissection of a 1771 map by Thomas Jefferys displaying the Old Bahama Channel as the Old Channel and the Great Bahama Bank as the Grand Bank of Bahama. (Source: US Library of Congress).

The Great Bahama Bank is about 50 miles (80 km) south of Bahama Island and the Little Bahama Bank. This bank forms much of the eastern boundary of the Bahama Channel and is penetrated by deep water gorges called the Tongue of the Ocean and the Exuma Sound further east of the channel.

The Great Bahama Bank covers an area of approximately 37,000 square miles (95,800 sq. km), almost seven times larger than the Little Bahama Bank. Its northern boundary extends eastward from the northern end of the Bimini chain (in the northwest Bahamas) for about 158 miles (255 km) to the northern end of Eleuthera Island at the Bank's northeastern end. The southern boundary of the Great Bahama Bank is over 193 miles long (311 km) from the western end of the Old Bahama Channel to the southeastern end of the Great Bahama Bank. Its western boundary stretches approximately 480 miles (772 km) in a south-north direction along the eastern border of the Bahama Channel.

The Little Bahama Bank is separated from the Great Bahama Bank by two adjacent channels in the northern Bahamas. These channels run roughly in an east-west and a northeast-southwest direction and are called the Northwest Providence Channel and the Northeast Providence Channel. The Northwest Providence Channel is immediately south of Grand Bahama Island, and the Northeast Providence Channel is south of Abaco Island, with its eastern end facing the Atlantic Ocean.

These channels are about 50 miles (80 km) wide, with three private cruise islands located along their northern and southern boundaries. Disney's Cruise Line's Castaway Cay is on the north side near south Abaco Island. Castaway Cay once carried the Spanish name Gorda Cay (meaning Fat or Thick Cay) before Disney purchased a 99-year lease in 1997 and renamed it. On the channels' south side is the Royal Caribbean International's CoCoCay, and the Norwegian Cruise Line's Great

Stirrup Cay. CoCoCay was named Little Stirrup's Cay before being changed to CoCoCay. (See Illustration 20).

After entering the New Bahama Channel, ships often navigated northward, passing the western entrance of the Northwest Providence Channel. On their return voyages to Spain, Spanish vessels occasionally transited the Northwest Providence and Northeast Providence Channels.[116] These deepwater gouges have a length of about 100 miles (160 km) from west to east and average about 50 miles (80 km) in width. They are equally hazardous to navigate due to their proximity to the Great and Little Bahama Banks' shallow waters.

Spanish conquistadors and governors shipped tons of gold, silver, emeralds, and other commodities to Spain during the conquests of Native American Empires through the Bahama Channel. Large quantities of silk, porcelain, and precious stones from India and China added to the bulk of goods shipped through the New Bahama Channel. These goods were exported from the Philippines to Mexico aboard Spanish "Manilla Galleons" sailing the Pacific Ocean from 1565 to 1815.[117]

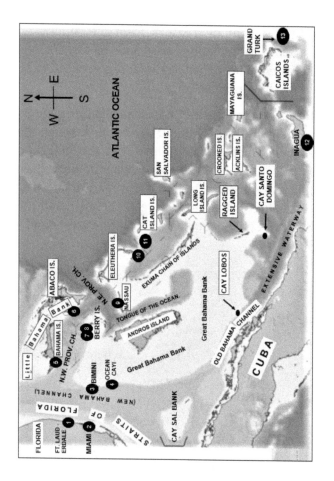

Illustration 20: Map displaying cruise ports in Florida, The Bahamas, and the Turks and Caicos Islands. 1: Port Fort Lauderdale (South Florida, USA); 2: Port Miami (South Florida, USA); 3: Port Bimini (Bimini, Bahamas); 4: Ocean Cay MSC Marine Reserve (Bimini Chain, Bahamas); 5: Port of Freeport (Grand Bahama Island, Bahamas); 6: Castaway Cay (West of South, Abaco Islands, Bahamas); 7: CocoCay (Berry Islands, Bahamas); 8: Great Stirrup Cay (Berry Islands, Bahamas); 9: Port Nassau (New Providence Island, Bahamas); 10: Port Princess Cays (South Eleuthera Island, Bahamas); 11: Half Moon Cay (Little San Salvador, Cat Island); 12: Matthew Town (Great Inagua Island, Bahamas); and 13: Grand Turk Cruise Center (Turks Island, Turks and Caicos Islands). (Source: Wikipedia. Names and ports inserted. Not to scale).

The transshipment of treasure from the Americas to Spain ended due to the depletion of precious metals and stones from Spanish mines and the independence revolutions in Spanish colonies in the Americas.

Over the ensuing centuries, Spanish navigators gained firsthand experience with the dangers of sea routes through the Old and New Bahama Channels. Countless lives and billions of dollars worth of treasure in today's money went down in these waters. Spanish ships making the annual trip rendezvoused at Havana, Cuba, to replenish supplies before departing northward for the New Bahama Channel during their homeward-bound voyages.

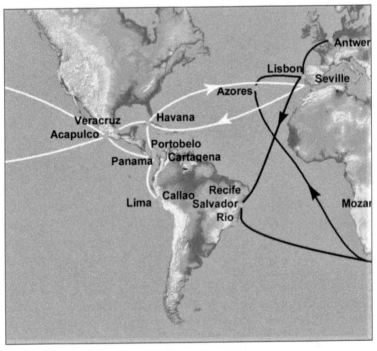

Illustration 21: Spanish galleons shipping routes (white arrows) from the Philippines to the Americas and from the Americas to Spain (Source: Wikipedia)

While en route to the Bahama Channel, these ships sailed north of Cay Sal (The Bahamas' western-most island) from Cuba. After entering the Bahama Channel, many ships, their crews, and cargoes met their demise in the shallow waters of the Little Bahama Bank due to inclement weather or navigational errors.[118] The wreck of the Spanish galleon Nuestra Señora de la Maravillas (Our Lady of Wonders) is a prime example of the dangers mariners encountered on the Little Bahama Bank.

The Nuestra Señora was en route to Spain in 1656 when it was caught in a winter storm. The vessel accidentally struck another ship that accompanied her, ran aground on the Little Bahama Bank, and sank in 30 feet (9 meters) of water. The Nuestra Señora was laden with 30 to 40 tons of gold, silver, emeralds, and other treasure.

The ship's captain attempted to avoid grounding on the Little Bahama Bank when the accident occurred.[119] The Spanish ship had left Vera Cruz, Mexico, stopped at Havana, and departed about two days before the incident near Memory Rock, about 20 miles (32 km) northwest of West End, Grand Bahama.[120]

The report that the Nuestra Señora was lost in shallow waters near "Isla de La Bahama" (or Bahama Island) would have been unforgettable in the minds of early explorers. Not only did news of such incidents spread through Western Europe, but reports reached the ears of wreckers living in the Bahama Colony. The Nuestra Señora wreck was found in 1986 and became the most significant find of its kind in the Western Hemisphere, with an estimated value of US$1.6 billion.[121]

A team of archaeologists and divers was led by American businessman Herbert Humphreys Jr. Months after the wreck, Spanish authorities attempted to salvage the sunken treasure with little success. Among the lost treasure was a golden statue of Madonna worth about $37 million.[122]

Pirates who hung out in Nassau Harbour were a threat to Spanish ships. Their Pirate Republic was a strategic base for launching attacks on European treasure ships and territories in the Caribbean region.[123] Disruption of the Spanish trade by pirates and Bahamian and Turks and Caicos Islander wreckers provoked the wrath of Spanish authorities in Cuba, who dispatched naval forces to burn settlements to the ground. Spanish authorities introduced annual naval escorts for their treasure vessels in the Pacific and Atlantic Oceans to stop the sea-robbers. On the Atlantic side, two fleets, each comprising 60 to 90 Spanish ships, arrived in the Americas annually.[124]

Surprisingly, most casualties experienced by Spanish vessels in the Americas were not due to pirate attacks or battles at sea with rival powers. According to Spanish researchers, an estimated 681 Spanish ships were lost with thousands of lives aboard. About 91 percent of the losses were due to storms and Hurricanes. [125] Only 1.4 percent of the overall loss was due to naval engagements, and 0.8 percent was the result of pirate attacks.

The first Spanish vessel lost in the "New World" was Columbus' flagship, the Santa Maria, in 1493, and the last Spanish vessel lost in the Americas was the Spanish destroyer Plutón. The Plutón was sunk by a US Navy vessel during the Spanish-American War in 1898.[126]

Spanish ships loaded with treasure were also lost on the Great Bahama Bank. Unconfirmed reports of the Spanish vessel Santiago El Grande state that this ship sank in the southern Bimini chain during a storm in 1765. Treasure hunter Rick Meyers said that the ship was believed to have 238 tons of silver and 2.5 tons of gold on board, "worth $3 billion in today's market." However, treasure found at the site to date paled compared to Meyers' claim.[127]

In September 2021, treasure hunters reportedly located thirteen Spanish wrecks in The Bahamas through satellite imagery, with one treasure ship believed to have about one billion dollars worth of treasure aboard. Additionally, some treasure hunters claim that "the second and third most valuable wrecks in the entire Western Hemisphere" are on the Little Bahama Bank.[128]

Spanish wrecks also occurred near the Old Bahama Channel or along the Extensive Waterway adjoining the Old Bahama Channel. For example, the Spanish galleon Nuestra Señora de la Pura y Limpia Concepción was caught in a storm while transiting this waterway en route to Spain from Cuba. The vessel suffered severe damage and was tossed onto the Silver Bank by strong winds near the eastern end of the waterway in 1641.[129] The ship had some $200 million in gold, silver, and jewels aboard.[130] The Silver Bank is about 60 miles (96 km) north of the Dominican Republic.

With such devastation, cartographers were minded to publish the names and locations of these banks and channels in official correspondence and on nautical charts. Charts that included the name "Bahama" would have subconsciously alerted Spanish mariners, mapmakers, and royal authorities to the grave dangers these "shallow waters" posed, thus adding to the fame (or infamy) of the name Bahama. Naturally, the awareness of the Bahama-named banks and channels grew as maritime traffic increased during the 1500s.

This writer believes that the (Little) Bahama Bank and the (New) Bahama Channel were among the first bodies of water where the name Bahama was applied. It is further believed that the name Bahama was later adopted for the Great Bahama Bank and the Old Bahama Channel due to their similarity in geographic features. The words Little, New, Great and Old would have been added to distinguish the two banks and channels from each other. More research is needed to determine the chronological order in which these banks and channels were named. Nevertheless, it is believed that the name

Bahama originated from the Lucayan Island that the Lucayans called Bahama.

Undoubtedly, the proximity of these channels and expansive banks to Bahama Island, the sinking of Spanish treasure ships on banks or in nearby channels of similar features, the resettling of the Bahama Islands (from 1648 onwards), the Golden Age of Piracy (1650 – 1730), and the invasions of these islands by rival European powers had all contributed to the adoption of the name "Bahama" for the New and Old Bahama Channels and the Great and Little Bahama Banks. Today, the Straits of Florida (Bahama Channel), Northwest Providence and Northeast Providence Channels, the Old Bahama Channel, and its Extended Waterway are primary passageways for cruise ships. Those who travel these waterways aboard cruise ships or commercial vessels have a unique opportunity to reflect on historical events that resulted in the naming of these channels and banks, giving birth to the nations of the modern Americas.

Chapter 9

From Bahama Channel to Straits of Florida (or Florida Straits)

The name Bahama was of common usage after it was applied to the large marine banks and channels during the 1500s. The Bahama Channel (also known as the New Bahama Channel) was the original name the Spanish gave this strategic waterway during the early European colonization of the Americas. This channel is located between Florida and the Bahama Islands. Chapter 8 highlighted how the name Bahama was likely applied to this channel after discovering it as an alternative route to Spain in 1519.

An early representation of the name Bahama is seen on Spanish historian Antonio de Herrera y Tordesillas' 1601 map *Yᵃˢ de los Lucayos* (Lucayan Islands) as Canal de Bahama (Bahama Channel).[131] However, during the late 1700s, the name Bahama Channel appeared on maps along with the names Gulf of Florida and Straits of Florida (Florida Straits).

Generally, a strait is a passage of water between landmasses connected to a larger body of water at each end. A channel is a wide strait. The two words (strait and channel) are often used interchangeably. The over 50-mile (80 km) wide Bahama Channel between Florida's east coast and The Bahamas'

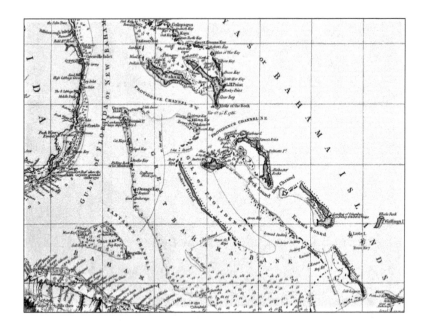

Illustration 22: A dissection of the 1803 map showing the Lucayan Islands as "Lucayas or Bahama Islands" by English cartographer Aaron Arrowsmith. Also shown are the Straits of Florida as the New Bahama Channel. (Source: Wikimedia).

western islands (Grand Bahama and Bimini) are considered a strait.

The narrower body of water between the Great Bahama Bank's southern boundary (near Cay Lobos) and central Cuba's northern coast also fits the description of a strait. This body of water was once named the Old Straits of Bahama[132] (Illustration 19) or the Old Channel[133] and is now called the Old Bahama Channel.

As time passed, various terms were used to describe the Bahama Channel. These terms included the New Bahama Channel, the Gulf of Florida, and now the Straits of Florida (or Florida Straits). The Florida Straits' western end lies between the Florida Keys and the northwestern coast of Cuba (near

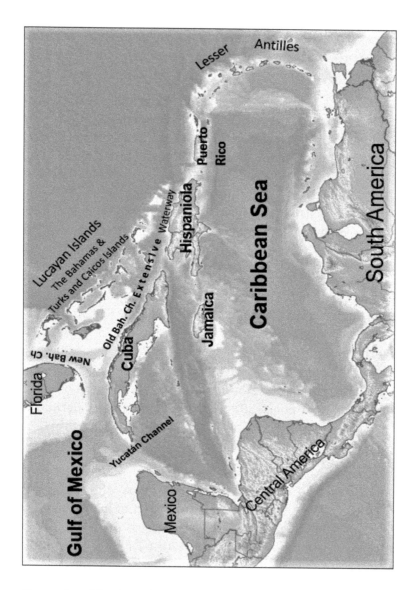

Illustration 23: Map displaying Old Bahama Channel's Extensive Waterway and the Caribbean Sea. (Source: Wikipedia. Names inserted).

Havana) and the opening of the Gulf of Mexico.[134] The Florida Straits extends eastward from Key West, Florida, following along the southern coasts of the Florida Keys. The Florida

79

Straits then turns northward along the Florida east coast, where that portion of the waterway was previously named the (New) Bahama Channel and connects with the Atlantic Ocean.

Ships transiting the strait from Mexico or Cuba also navigated between the Florida Keys and the Cay Sal Bank (in the western Bahamas). Cay Sal Bank is 130 miles (209 km) northeast of Havana, Cuba, and 90 miles (144 km) southeast of Key West, about halfway between Cuba's northwest coast and the Florida Keys. Immediately south of the Bank is the Nicholas Channel, and to the east of the Bank is the Santaren Channel. Bronze cannons have been reportedly sighted on a reef on this bank and are believed to belong to a Spanish treasure ship.[135]

After passing Cay Sal, Spanish vessels continued northward, passing between Florida and the islands in the northwestern Bahamas, before altering course for Spain. The width of the Straits of Florida varies between 60 (96 km) and 90 miles (144 km). The full length of the Florida Straits is about 300 miles (482 km) from its western end to its northern end.[136] Its north end lies between the Florida mainland (in the area of Port St. Lucie, about 50 miles (80 km) north of Palm Beach, Florida) and the northwestern end of the Little Bahama Bank, north of Grand Bahama.

A warm-water current flows out of the Gulf of Mexico through the Florida Straits called the Gulf Stream. After exiting the Florida Straits, the Gulf Stream forms part of the Atlantic Gyre system. The Stream flows eastward across the North Atlantic Ocean, creating warmer temperatures. The Gulf Stream then travels southward along Europe's and North Africa's west coasts before flowing westward into the Caribbean region and back into the Gulf of Mexico, repeating the cycle.

Illustration 24: Map showing Cay Sal Bank. (Source: Wikipedia. Names inserted)

As Spanish colonies grew and became more entrenched in North America, military and commercial activities increased around Florida.[137] Spain founded its first colony, St. Augustine, in what is now continental America in 1565.[138] St. Augustine is the United States' oldest city, founded by European colonists.

The Spanish annual transpacific shipment of goods and supplies from the Philippines to Mexico began in 1565, adding to the Florida maritime traffic.[139] Additionally, British interests in Florida intensified after occupying the Peninsula from 1763 to 1784.

From 1537 to 1800, Spain operated its treasure fleet system, providing naval escort for numerous treasure ships transporting goods to and from the Americas.[140] Many Spanish ships were lost to storms, accidents, or incidents of naval engagements near the Florida coast during their return voyages.[141]

The Florida Straits were the first leg of a Spanish ship's voyage departing Cuba for Spain through the (New) Bahama Channel. The Florida Keys, like the Little Bahama Bank, became the graveyard for numerous Spanish ships that ran aground in Florida's shallow waters with tons of treasure aboard.

For example, in 1622, the Señora de Atocha sank in a hurricane near Key West, Florida.[142] During the early 1970s, American treasure hunter Mel Fisher found over $400 million worth of sunken treasure from this vessel. Another example of Spanish wrecks in the Florida area was the Nuestra España fleet.

This fleet comprising three galleons and 18 ships was caught in a violent hurricane off Florida's south coast after departing Havana in 1733. The storm destroyed the vessels and widely scattered them among the Florida Keys.[143]

Increased commercial and military activities around Florida would have brought widespread attention to Florida by Spanish authorities, especially as Spanish colonization of the Florida Peninsula continued to expand, thereby popularizing its name. Of note is that the name Gulf (or Straits) of Florida began appearing with the name Bahama (or New Bahama) Channel on European maps during the 1700s (and throughout the 1800s).

As European colonists discovered wealth and staked their claims on America's mainland, the Bahama Islands became less relevant to their economic and political interests. This writer believes that Florida's colonization, increased maritime traffic, and shipwrecks around the peninsula contributed to the name Florida Gulf (or Straits) becoming preferred by European authorities, eventually replacing the name (New) Bahama Channel.

Today, this Spanish-derived name (Florida) represents a landmass approximately ten times the Bahama Islands' size and covers all waters between Florida and The Bahamas. Nevertheless, the name Bahama most likely remained a cautionary warning whenever mariners saw the name on nautical charts while sailing near these islands' banks and channels.

Despite the name change, it would be historically and geographically appropriate for Bahamians to reclaim this lost maritime heritage (either formally or informally) by naming or calling the portion of the Florida Straits that falls under The Bahamas' maritime jurisdiction the "New Bahama Channel." This reclamation would shed fresh light on a long-forgotten aspect of the Americas' founding.

Chapter 10

Summing Up How The Bahamas Got its Name

Discovering how name changes came about in the Lucayan Islands reveals an exciting story of how these islands shaped the Americas' early history. Name changes in the Americas began in the Lucayan Islands. The Lucayan Islands were originally named by the Lucayans and their ancestors about 800 years or more before Columbus set foot on these islands.

However, these names began to change shortly after Columbus' historic Atlantic Ocean crossing, resulting in the European colonization of the Ancient World of the Western Hemisphere. The Lucayan Islands were among the first landmasses to be renamed, followed by the Caribbean Islands, and then the wider Americas. Thus began the naming or renaming of many islands, archipelagos, regions, continents, and waters within the Americas.

Within two weeks of Columbus' landfall, Columbus had renamed several of the central and southern Lucayan Islands he visited or sighted, starting with Guanahani, the island of his first landfall. Columbus claimed the island for the Spanish Crown and called it San Salvador, making it the first landmass to be renamed by Europeans in the Americas. Though the Spanish never settled the Lucayan Islands, they did sail through Lucayan waters in transit to the wider Americas or during their return voyages to Spain. Such voyages acquainted the Spanish with these islands' indigenous names throughout the chain.

As the English, French, and Dutch invaded the Spanish domain in the Americas, the indigenous names among the islands and mainland in the wider Americas began to change, reflecting the colonial presence of each rival power and their latest territorial claims. As indicated in Chapter 3, Las Islas de Los Lucayos was the first name given to the Lucayan Islands as a single archipelago comprising The Bahama and the Turks and Caicos Islands. Interestingly, this name is still used today in its English form (Lucayan Islands) among English speakers.

Because The Bahamas and Turks and Caicos Islands are separate countries within the Lucayan Archipelago, they are individually described as the Bahama Archipelago and the Turks and Caicos Islands Archipelago. Despite European territorial claims among these islands, the names of many of these islands have retained their indigenous roots. Additionally, indigenous names were found in these countries' official titles. This is also the case for several countries within the Caribbean region, such as Cuba, Haiti, and Jamaica, which all have Taino roots like the name Bahama.

The native names for other countries like Puerto Rico (original Taino name, Borinquén)[144] and Hispaniola (Taino name Ayiti) were renamed with Spanish names. The name for the Bahama Archipelago was changed on at least three occasions before being officially named "The Commonwealth of The Bahamas" upon attaining independence in 1973.[145]

Granberry's and Vescelius' observation that the name Bahama was an indigenous name for today's Grand Bahama Island is fundamental to discovering how The Bahamas got its name.

Illustration 25: Map of The Bahamas (source: Wikipedia)

As stated in Chapter 8, it is believed that the name Bahama was adopted and applied to the large marine banks (Great and Little Bahama Banks) and channels (Old and New Bahama Channels) before being appended to the entire Bahama chain of islands on maps. However, the chronological order in which the name Bahama was applied to the banks, channels, and island chain will require more research.

It is plausible that the name Bahama was first applied to the bank (the Little Bahama Bank) adjacent to Grand Bahama and later to the adjacent channel (the New Bahama Channel) or vice versa. The name Bahama might have then been applied to the larger bank (the Great Bahama Bank) and the southern channel (the Old Bahama Channel) before being formally adopted for the entire Bahama chain.

It is also reasonable to believe that the name Bahama might have been permanently appended to the Turks and Caicos Islands at the southern end of the Lucayan chain had these islands not been settled by a separate group of English colonists from Bermuda. This group was not interested in the Bahama group of settlers being in charge of Turks and Caicos Islands' affairs.

In making a case for how The Bahamas got its name, the following points are noted:

- Columbus was the first European to encounter the Lucayans within the Lucayan chain of islands;
- Columbus was the first European to discover the channel on Cuba's north coast (now called the Old Bahama Channel) after departing the Lucayan Islands in 1492;
- Columbus was the first European to navigate the Extensive Waterway adjoining the eastern end of the old (Bahama) channel in making his way to Hispaniola before returning to Spain in 1493;
- the Spanish began colonizing Hispaniola in 1493 and initiated the conquest of Cuba in 1511, which gave the Spanish access to the old (Bahama) channel;
- the old (Bahama) channel and its Extensive Waterway (or parts thereof) became a main passageway for Spanish ships returning to Spain before the New Bahama Channel was discovered;
- the name Bahama was not applied to the old (Bahama) channel until after the new (Bahama) channel adjacent

to (Grand) Bahama Island in the north was discovered in 1519.

It is further noted:

- the name Bahama is the Taino name for today's Grand Bahama Island before European contact;
- the existence of the Lucayan Island named Bahama became known to the Spanish sometime after 1493 (Columbus' second voyage to the Americas) and before 1513 (the year Ponce de León completed his expedition to Florida);
- Ponce de León's 1513 journey took him northward from Puerto Rico along the entire eastern and northwestern seaboards of the Lucayos (from Grand Turk Island in the south to Bahama Island and Bimini in the northwest);
- Ponce de León was one of the first known Spaniards in recorded history to sail across the (New) Bahama Channel to Florida's east coast from the northwestern Bahamas, facilitating an initial acquaint with the channel by Europeans;
- the Florida expedition took Ponce de León from Florida to the northwest coast of Cuba, showing the geographic connection between the (New) Bahama Channel and the waters off Havana, Cuba;
- Hernán Cortés' Chief pilot, Anton de Alaminos, had accompanied Ponce de León on his expedition to Florida in 1513, thus becoming aware of the channel's existence and connection with Cuba's waters;
- Anton discovered for the first time that the (New) Bahama Channel could be used as a return route to Spain during his escape from Cuba to Spain in 1519;
- the (New) Bahama Channel became a primary route for Spanish ships returning to Spain after 1519;

Considering that:

- Bahama Island is adjacent to the northern end of the (New) Bahama Channel;
- Bahama Island is also at the southwestern corner of the relatively large bank (now named the Little Bahama Bank);
- mariners occasionally used Bahama Island as a navigational reference point when passing through the (new) Bahama channel, thus acquainting mariners with the name Bahama;
- ships transited the (new) Bahama channel laden with large hauls of treasure and were sometimes destroyed by storms, resulting in the loss of numerous Spanish lives in the channel or on the Little Bahama Bank;
- the similarities in geographical features of the larger bank (the Great Bahama Bank) to the Little Bahama Bank and the (new) Bahama channel to the channel in the south (the Old Bahama Channel) resulted in these maritime areas being named the Great Bahama Bank and the Old Bahama Channel;
- the names Great and Little and New and Old were probably added later to these banks and channels to distinguish them from each other;
- the association of the name Bahama with the Great Bahama Bank and the Old Bahama Channel would have added to the universal acceptance of the name Bahama for the general area.

Noting that:

- the Spanish did not find any gold, precious stones, spices, or other valuable commodities in the Lucayan Islands;
- Spanish interests in the Lucayan Islands had fallen off after these islands became depleted of their Lucayan slave labor during the 1520s;

- European economic priorities in the Americas shifted away from the Caribbean region to Central and South America after vast quantities of gold and other natural resources were discovered in these regions during the early 1500s;
- English authorities initially identified the Lucayan Islands as "Buhama [Bahama] in America ...."[146] and not Lucayos upon resettling them in 1648, perhaps reinforcing the use of the name Bahama;
- The infestation of pirates in these islands during the Golden Age of Piracy would have helped spread the name Bahama throughout European countries that were colonizing the Caribbean region and the American mainland;
- Usage of the Spanish name Las Islas de Los Lucayos to identify these islands was probably less favored by their English colonists, whose motherland (England) was often at war with Spain;

Therefore, it can be concluded that:

- The Lucayan Island named Bahama is the same island as today's Grand Bahama Island;
- the name Bahama Island and its proximity to the Little Bahama Bank and the New Bahama Channel would have influenced cartographers to adopt the name Bahama for the Little Bahama Bank and the New Bahama Channel as navigational reference points;
- the name Bahama was later appended to the Great Bahama Bank and Old Bahama Channel due to their similarities in geographic features to the Little Bahama Bank and the New Bahama Channel;
- navigating through or near the channels and expansive banks with the name Bahama and the subsequent loss of ships, lives, and treasure in these channels or on

these banks helped brand the island chain as the Bahama Islands;

- The Turks and Caicos Islands settling by a separate group of Bermudan colonists resulted in this group of islands not being included under the name Bahama.

In summary, it is believed that the appendage of the name Bahama to the Lucayan Islands' banks and channels and the maritime activities around them resulted in British colonists adopting the name Bahama for these islands. As time progressed, the name Bahama gradually replaced Lucayos on maps.

The name Bahama was eventually formalized by British authorities after the Bahama Islands transitioned from proprietary governance to becoming a British Crown colony. This transition occurred after Captain Woodes Rogers, the Bahama Colony's first Royal Governor, was appointed in 1718.

During the colonial period, the plural form of the name Bahama (Bahamas), which represents all the Bahama Islands, was used and permanently included in these islands' official name after Great Britain granted the Bahama Colony independence in 1973. Today, the Commonwealth of The Bahamas is the official name of the Bahama Archipelago.

Chapter 11

The Final Analysis

The Bahamas and Turks and Caicos are two countries within the Lucayan Archipelago. The names of islands among these islands are either of Lucayan, Spanish, or English origin. Unlike the Americas, a name of European origin, the name Lucayan Islands or the Lucayan Archipelago was derived from the indigenous name for these islands' inhabitants (Lukku Cairi, meaning Island People).

Today, the Bahama Islands is a sovereign state officially named The Commonwealth of The Bahamas. These islands are generally referred to as The Bahamas, the Bahama Islands, the Islands of The Bahamas, New Providence and the Family Islands, or New Providence and the Out Islands.

Evidence strongly suggests that the name Bahamas is of Lucayan origin. This writer believes that the name Bahamas is of Taino-Lucayan origin, derived from the Lucayan Island, Bahama (now Grand Bahama), whose name was later applied to neighboring banks and channels due to maritime activities in the area. However, the popular thinking among some is that this name was derived from the Spanish words "baja mar" meaning "shallow water"[147] or "low sea."

In blending its indigenous and modern perspectives , the name Bahama could be described as a Taino-Lucayan name that carries a Spanish meaning in the minds of some. The Spanish origin is further strengthened by Spain's usage of the letter "h" (as in Bahama) and its historical significance in the Spanish language. However, the letter 's' in the word Bahamas was introduced during the English colonial period and later formalized on the occasion of The Bahamas' independence, representing one nation with many islands.

On the other hand, the Turks and Caicos Islands present a mix of European influence on the "Turks" side and indigenous influence on the "Caicos" side. The Turks and Caicos Islands were also settled by a separate group of Bermudans from those who colonized the Bahama Colony. This difference cultivated a sense of autonomy among the Turks and Caicos Islanders, who established a distinct identity for themselves.

Today, the Turks and Caicos Islands remain under the administration of Great Britain, with internal self-rule. These islands are classified as a British Overseas Territory and are officially named the Turks and Caicos Islands. Despite their differences, the Turks and Caicos Islands and The Bahamas belong to the same archipelago whose inhabitants share a common history, geography, and culture with Bahamians.

Though The Bahamas and Turks and Caicos Islands were politically separated in 1973, both countries still share a common geographical, historical, and cultural bond. This common bond is forever sealed by the Lucayan Archipelago in which Bahamians and Turks and Caicos Islanders live and by the waters that encompass it, which hopefully will be named the Lucayan Sea.

Timeline Relevant to Name Changes on European Maps of the Americas

11,000 years ago: The land bridge (Beringia) between East Asia and the northern continent of the Ancient World of the Western Hemisphere (now North America) was submerged by seawater after the last ice age. Rising seawater levels prevented the overland migration of the Paleoindians from Asia to the Americas.

1492 – 1538: The Americas remained nameless as a continental group in the Western Hemisphere.

700 AD: The Lucayan ancestors from Hispaniola began settling in the southern Lucayan Islands.

12 October 1492: Italian explorer Christopher Columbus made his first landfall in the Ancient World of the Western Hemisphere on the Lucayan Island named Guanahani, which he renamed San Salvador.

12 October 1492: The Old World of Europe accidentally encountered the Ancient World of the Western Hemisphere upon Columbus' arrival in Lucayan waters; thus began the unfolding of the modern nations of the Americas.

1493: Columbus navigates through the channel between the Great Bahama Bank and Cuba's north coast, which became known as the Old Channel (or Old Bahama Channel).

Early 1500s: The name Los Islas de Los Lucayos or (Las Islas de Las Lucayas) began appearing on maps, representing the entire Lucayan chain of Islands.

1501: Italian explorer Amerigo Vespucci realizes that Columbus discovered a world that was new to contemporary European explorers.

1507: The southern continent in the Western Hemisphere was named America by German cartographer Martin Waldseemüller in honor of Italian explorer Amerigo Vespucci.

1513: During his voyage to Florida, Ponce de León encounters the Turks Island and records it as belonging to the "Lucayos."

1513: Ponce de León and Anton de Alaminos were the first Europeans to make landfall in Florida. The explorers had sailed the entire length of the Lucayan chain of islands before crossing a waterway that later became known as the Bahama Channel (or New Bahama Channel) to reach Florida.

1519: The New Bahama Channel was fully navigated for the first time by Europeans during Anton de Alaminos return trip to Spain from Cuba.

1519: The first township was founded in Havana in northwestern Cuba.

1519 – 1800: Spanish treasure fleets navigated through the New Bahama Channel during their return trip to Spain.

1500s - 1800: Spanish ships periodically ran aground on the Great and Little Bahama Banks after departing Cuba. The groundings were due to storms or poor navigation.

1538: The name America was also applied to North America by the Belgian mapmaker Gerardus Mercator.

1565: The permanent colonization of the Florida Peninsula began near Saint Augustine, Florida, by Pedro Menéndez de Avilés, the Spanish Governor and Adelantado of Florida.

By the early 1600s: The Lucayan Islands are identified on maps as Los Lucayos (or Las Lucayas).

By the early 1600s: The name Bahama Channel (or New Bahama Channel) is identified on maps.

1648: The English Crown granted a license to the English Bermudan group known as the Eleutheran Adventurers to settle the Bahama Islands.

1670s: A separate group of Bermudans began settling in the southern Lucayan Islands known as the Turks and Caicos Islands.

1670s: The Bahama Islands were administered by English Lords Proprietors who appointed a governor to manage the islands in their absence.

1700s: The name Gulf of Florida (or Straits of Florida) is shown alongside the name Bahama Channel (or New Bahama Channel).

1700s: The name Bahama Islands is displayed alongside the name Lucayos.

1704 – 1717: The Bahama Islands were left without a proprietary governor.

1706 – 1718: Pirates of the Caribbean claimed Nassau as a Republic of the Pirates.

1718: English Captain Woodes Rogers took up office as the Bahama Islands' first Royal Governor and drove the pirates out of the islands.

By the late 1700s: The name Gulf of Florida (Straits of Florida) is displayed alongside Bahama Channel or by itself.

1800: Spanish ended its transshipments of treasure from the Americas to Spain.

Mid-1800s – Early 1900s: The name Bahama Islands replaces the name Lucayan Islands on maps.

1848: The Turks Island group and the Caicos Islands group were officially identified under a single name as the Turks and Caicos Islands and granted internal self-rule under the British Jamaica Colony.

1962: The Turks and Caicos Islands administration was placed under the Bahama Island Colony after Jamaica was granted its independence.

1969: The Bahama Colony adopted the name The Commonwealth of the Bahama Islands.

1973: The Bahama Colony was granted independence by Great Britain and was officially named The Commonwealth of The Bahamas. The Turks and Caicos Islands was made a British Crown colony with an appointed governor.

About the Author

Commodore (retired) Tellis A. Bethel Sr. was born in Nassau, where he spent his early childhood on the "Fort Hill" near Fort Fincastle in Grants Town. He is a descendant of Eleuthera, Long Island, and Grand Bahama. He currently heads The Bahamas' Security Forces Inspectorate at the Ministry of National Security and is a former Commander of the Royal Bahamas Defence Force.

As a young man, Commodore Bethel was keenly interested in the great outdoors, where he enjoyed scuba diving, private and ultralight aircraft flying, and sky diving. He had also worked as a bellboy aboard the S/S Emerald Seas, a popular cruise ship of its day that was previously used as a World War II troop transport vessel.

Commodore Bethel was later employed in the operations department of one of the world's largest shipping companies (Navios) before joining the Royal Bahamas Defence Force as a naval officer in 1981. Commodore Bethel resigned from the Force in 1991 and rejoined five years later in 1996, eventually becoming the Commander Defence Force.

He has served in junior and senior command posts in the Defence Force's sea-going patrol squadron, bases, and at

Defence Headquarters. Commodore Bethel was involved in some of the Force's largest maritime law enforcement operations and drug busts during peak years of the South American-US drug trade during the 1980s. Under his watch as Commander Defence Force, the Defence Force hosted or engaged in some of the most extensive regional military training exercises, capital development projects, and modernization programs in the Force's history.

Commodore Bethel is a graduate of Saint John's College in Nassau, the UK's Britannia Royal Naval College, the US Naval War College's Naval Staff College, and York St. John University in England. He holds a master's degree in Leading Innovation and Change from York St. John University, England, and has attended renowned military and civil-military institutions in Asia, the United States, Europe, and the Caribbean.

He enjoys writing and sharing insights on The Bahamas' and Turks and Caicos Islands' rich heritage and has become a leading proponent of naming the unnamed waters of both countries the Lucayan Sea. He is the author of the trilogy Lucayan Sea: A Case For Naming the Historic Waters Of The Bahamas And Turks And Caicos Islands. Commodore Bethel and his wife, Teri, have two adult sons.

References

[1] https://en.wikipedia.org/wiki/Lucayan_Archipelago [Retrieved 9 June, 2014].

[2] Smith, Jean Reeder and Smith, Baldwin Lacey. (1980). *Essentials of World History*. New York: Barron's Educational Series, Inc. p.iii. See also: Duncan, Marcel. (1964). *Larousse Encyclopedia of Modern History, From 1500 to the Present Day*. New York: Harper and Row.

[3] Smith, Jean Reeder and Smith, Lacey Baldwin (1980). Essentials of World History. London: Barron Educational Series, pp.76-77.

[4] https://www.britannica.com/event/Middle-Ages [Retrieved: 17 January 2021].

[5] Kamen, Henry. (2005). *Spain 1469-1714* (3rd Ed.). New York: Pearson/Longman. p. 29.

[6] https://www.merriam-webster.com/dictionary/eastern%20hemisphere [Retrieved: 17 January, 2021].

[7] https://www.newyorker.com/culture/culture-desk/canadas-impossible-acknowledgment [Retrieved: 17 January 2021].

[8] Keegan, William F., et al. (Eds.). (2013). The Oxford Handbook of Caribbean Archaeology. New York: Oxford University Press. p. 264.

[9] https://www.loc.gov/item/73697197/ [Retrieved 10 June 2020].

[10] https://www.geraceresearchcentre.com/pdfs/14thNatHist/197-211_Gnivecki.pdf [Retrieved 10 June 2020].

[11] Craton, Michael and Saunders, Gail. (1999). Islanders in the Stream: A History of the Bahamian People-From Aboriginal Times to the End of Slavery. Georgia: University of Georgia Press. p. 26.

[12] Riley, Sandra. (2000). Homeward Bound: A History of the Bahama Islands to 1850 with a Definitive Study of Abaco In the American Loyalist Plantation Period. Florida: Riley Hall Publishers. p. 16.

[13] https:/brill.com//view/book/edcoll/9789004273689/BP000002.xml?language=en [Retrieved 5 Jan 2021]

[14] https://www.nationsencyclopedia.com/Americas/United-Kingdom-American-Dependencies-TURKS-AND-CAICOS-ISLANDS.html [Retrieved 20 January 2021].

[15] https://suntci.com/discrediting-the-myth-tci-dependent-or-not-p5671129.htm [Retrieved: 20 January 2021].

[16] De Booy, T. (1918). The Turks and Caicos Islands, British West Indies. Geographical Review, 6(1), 37-51. doi:10.2307/207448.

[17] https://www.visittci.com/nature-and-history/flora-and-fauna/turks-head-cacti [Retrieved 20 January 2021].

[18] Aceto, Michael and Williams, Jeffrey Payne. (Eds.). (2003). *Contact Englishes of the Eastern Caribbean*. Amsterdam: John Benjamin Publishing Company. p. 51.

[19] https://turksandcaicostourism.com/about-turks-and-caicos [Retrieved 20 January 2021].

[20] https://www.visittci.com/nature-and-history/history/pirates-in-the-turks-and-caicos [Retrieved 20 January 2021].

[21] https://turksandcaicostourism.com/about-turks-and-caicos/ [Retrieved 20 January 2021].

[22] Keegan, William F. and Carlson, Lisabeth A. (2008). *Talking Taino: Caribbean Natural History from a Native Perspective*. Alabama: University of Alabama Press. p. 10.

[23] Keegan, William F. and Carlson, Lisabeth A. (2008). Talking Taino: Caribbean Natural History from a Native Perspective. Alabama: University of Alabama Press. p.11.

[24] Keegan, William F. and Carlson, Lisabeth A. (2008). Talking Taino: Caribbean Natural History from A Native Perspective. Alabama: University of Alabama Press.pp.11-12.

[25] Keegan, William F. and Carlson, Lisabeth A. (2008). Talking Taino: Caribbean Natural History from a Native Perspective. Alabama: University of Alabama Press. p.11.

[26] Scisco. L. (1913). The Track of Ponce de Leon in 1513. Bulletin of the American Geographical Society, 45(10), 721-735. Doi:10.2307/200163.

[27] Sauer, Carl Ortwin. (1966). *The Early Spanish Main*. New York: Cambridge University Press. p. 1.

[28] Little, Benerson. (2007). The Buccaneer's Realm: Pirate Life on the Spanish Main, 1674-1688. Washington: Potomac Book Inc. p. 2.

[29] Sauer, Carl Ortwin. (1966). *The Early Spanish Main*. New York: Cambridge University Press. p. 1.

[30] Sauer, Carl Ortwin. (1966). *The Early Spanish Main*. New York: Cambridge University Press. p. 1.

[31] https://www.orlandosentinel.com/news/os-xpm-1987-10-11-0150250123-story.html [Retrieved 10 June 2020].

[32] Sauer, Carl Ortwin. (1966). The Early Spanish Main. New York: Cambridge University Press. pp.3-4.

[33] Sauer, Carl Ortwin. (1966). The Early Spanish Main. New York: Cambridge University Press. pp.3-4.

[34] Sauer, Carl Ortwin (1966) The Early Spanish Main. Los Angeles: University of California Press. pp.1-2.

[35] https://www.biography.com/explorer/amerigo-vespucci [Retrieved 10 June 2020].

[36] https://www.britannica.com/biography/Roderick [Retrieved 5 June 2020].

[37] Little, Benerson. (2007). *The Buccaneer's Realm: Pirate Life on the Spanish Main, 1674-1688.* Washington: Potomac Book Inc. p. 2.

[38] https://suntci.com/discrediting-the-myth-tci-dependent-or-not-p5671129.htm [Retrieved: 20 January 2021].

[39] Riley, Sandra. (2000). *Homeward Bound: A History of the Bahama Islands to 1850 with a Definitive Study of Abaco In the American Loyalist Plantation Period.* Florida: Riley Hall Publishers. pp. 26-27.

[40] https://quod.lib.umich.edu/e/eebo2/B20578.0001.001?rgn=main;view=fulltext [Retrieved 10 June 2020].

[41] Riley, Sandra. (2000). *Homeward Bound: A History of the Bahama Islands to 1850 with a Definitive Study of Abaco in the American Loyalist Plantation Period.* Miami: Riley Hall Publishers. p. 37.

[42] Bethell, Talbot. (2008). The Early Settlers of the Bahamas and Colonists of North America. Maryland: Heritage Books. pp. 65-66.

[43] https://bs.vlex.com/vid/the-bahama-constitution-order-council-42456981 [Retrieved 10 June 2020].

[44] CO/23/9 Folio 109, 31 March, 1779. Dept. of Archives, Nassau, Bahamas.

[45] https://www.britannica.com/place/The-Bahamas/Independence [Retrieved 10 June 2020].

[46] https://www.collinsdictionary.com/dictionary/spanish-english/bajamar [Retrieved: 20 April 2020].

[47] https://www.telegraph.co.uk/travel/destinations/caribbean/bahamas/articles/amazing-facts-about-the-bahamas/ [Retrieved 20 April 2020].

[48] McMorran, Jennifer. (2000). The Islands of The Bahamas. Quebec: Ulysse Travel Guides. p.22.

[49] Granberry, Julian and Vescelius, Gary S. (2004). *Languages of the Pre-Columbian Antilles.* Alabama: The University of Alabama Press, pp. 80-86.

[50] Granberry, Julian and Vescelius, Gary S. (2004). *Languages of the Pre-Columbian Antilles.* Alabama: The University of Alabama Press. pp. xiii-xiv.

[51] Granberry, Julian and Vescelius, Gary S. (2004). *Languages of the Pre-Columbian Antilles*. Alabama: The University of Alabama Press. pp. 69-71.

[52] Granberry, Julian and Vescelius, Gary S. (2004). *Languages of the Pre-Columbian Antilles*. Alabama: The University of Alabama Press. p. 82.

[53] Fernández, Gonzalo de Oviedo y Valdés. (1851). *Historia general y natural de las Indias - Volume 1*. Madrid: La Real Academia De La Historia. p. 25.

[54] Markham, Clements R. (1902). *Life of Christopher Columbus*. Liverpool: G. Philip & Son, Limited. p. 92.

[55] Dor-Ner, Zvi and Scheller, William G. (1992). Columbus and The Age of Discovery. New York: HarperCollins.p.155.

[56] Moralejo, A. (1977). *La "J" española y la "J" arábiga: Alfajarín y otros topónimos. Vol. 20-21*. Zaragoza: Archivo de filología aragonesa. pp. 319-322.

[57] https://en.wikipedia.org/wiki/Baja_California [Retrieved 10 June 2020].

[58] https://en.wikipedia.org/wiki/Baja_California [Retrieved 10 June 2020].

[59] Sandys, John E. (1910). *A Companion to Latin Studies*. Chicago: University of Chicago Press. pp. 811–812.

[60] Douglass, R. Thomas. (Dec. 1987). The Letter H in Spanish. Texas: Hispania, 70(4), 949-951.

[61] Douglass, R. Thomas. (Dec. 1987). The Letter H in Spanish. *Texas: Hispania, 70(4)*, 949-951.

[62] Douglass, R. Thomas. (Dec. 1987). The Letter H in Spanish. *Texas: Hispania 70(4)*, 949-951.

[63] Fernández, Gonzalo de Oviedo y Valdés. (1851). *Historia general y natural de las Indias - Volume 1*. Madrid: La Real Academia De La Historia. p. 25.

[64] Douglass, R. Thomas. (Dec. 1987). The Letter H in Spanish. *Texas: Hispania, 70(4)*, 949-951.

[65] http://www.cubadebate.cu/especiales/2019/02/04/las-palabras-tainas-que-usas-todos-los-dias-sin-darte-cuenta/#.X0scdshKjIU [Retrieved 10 June 2020].

[66] http://www.cubadebate.cu/especiales/2019/02/04/las-palabras-tainas-que-usas-todos-los-dias-sin-darte-cuenta/#.X0scdshKjIU [Retrieved 10 June 2020].

[67] Elsayed, R. (2018). *La presencia del arabismo en la antroponimia hispánica contemporánea*. Madrid: Universidad Complutense. p. 273.

[68] https://www.spanishdict.com/guide/spanish-vowels {Retrieved 10 June 2020].

[69] Granberry, Julian and Vescelius, Gary S. (2004). Languages of the Pre-Columbian Antilles. Alabama: The University of Alabama Press, pp. 80-86.

[70] https://www.geraceresearchcentre.com/pdfs/14thNatHist/197-211_Gnivecki.pdf [Retrieved 10 June 2020].

[71] Keegan, William F. and Carlson, Lisabeth A. (2008). Talking Taino: Caribbean Natural History from a Native Perspective. Alabama: University of Alabama Press. pp. 7-8.

[72] Keegan, William F., Hofman, Corinne L., and Rodriguez, Ramos Reniel. (Eds.) (2013). The Oxford Handbook of Caribbean Archaeology. Oxford: Oxford University Press, p. 275.

[73] http://www.thebahamasweekly.com/publish/bahamas-historical-society/Lucayan_Topynyms9510.shtml [Retrieved 10 June 2020].

[74] http://www.bahamapundit.com/2013/07/exploring-the-lucayan-prehistory-of-the-bahamas.html [Retrieved 21 September, 2013].

[75] Keegan, William F. and Carlson, Lisabeth A. (2008). *Talking Taino: Caribbean Natural History from a Native Perspective*. Alabama: University of Alabama Press. p. 11.

[76] https://www.loc.gov/item/73697197/ [Retrieved 20 August 2016].

[77] Loven, Sven. (2010). *Origins of the Tainan Culture, West Indies*. Alabama: University of Alabama Press. p. 57.

[78] http://digitalcollections.fiu.edu/tequesta/files/1948/48_1_05.pdf [Retrieved 10 June 2020].

[79] Keegan, William F., Hofman, Corinne L. and Rodriguez, Reniel R. (Eds.). (2013). *The Oxford Handbook of Caribbean Archaeology*. Oxford: Oxford University Press. p. 11.

[80] https://www.loc.gov/item/2010593321/ [Retrieved 10 June 2020].

[81] Fernández, Gonzalo de Oviedo y Valdés. (1851). *Historia general y natural de las Indias - Volume 1*. Madrid: La Real Academia De La Historia. p. 25.
https://commons.wikimedia.org/wiki/File:1818_Pinkerton_Map_of_the_West_Indies,_Antilles,_and_Caribbean_Sea_-_Geographicus_-_WestIndies2-pinkerton-1818.jpg [Retrieved 10 June 2020].

[82] Barratt, Peter. (2011). Bahama Saga: The epic saga of the Bahama Islands. Indiana: 1stBooks.pp.327-328.

[83] Barratt, Peter. (2011). Bahama Saga: The epic saga of the Bahama Islands. Indiana: 1st Books.pp.327-328.

84

https://www.loc.gov/resource/g3291s.ct000341/?r=0.595,0.284,0.118,0.0 45,0 [Retrieved 20 May 2020].

[85] National Maritime Historical Society & Sea History Magazine. (Nov 30, 2011). Sea History 137. Winter 2011-2012. New York: pp. 34-35.

[86] https://www.loc.gov/item/2003620053/ [Retrieved 20 May 2020].

87

https://www.loc.gov/resource/g3702c.ct011227/?r=0.074,1.079,0.994,0.3 75,0 [Retrieved 20 May 2020].

88

https://www.loc.gov/resource/g4980.ar174900/?r=0.476,0.556,0.286,0.10 8,0 [Retrieved 20 May 2020].

[89] https://www.loc.gov/resource/g3932c.ar160803/?r=0.189,-0.021,0.525,0.198,0 [Retrieved 20 May 2020].

[90] https://www.loc.gov/resource/g4980.ar175000/?r=-0.093,0.12,1.079,0.442,0 [Retrieved 20 May 2020].

91

https://www.loc.gov/resource/g4980.ar175000/?r=0.165,0.278,0.134,0.05 1,0 [Retrieved 20 May 2020].

[92] https://www.floridamuseum.ufl.edu/histarch/research/dominican-republic/la-isabela/ [Retrieved 4 April 2020].

[93] https://www.britannica.com/place/Havana/History [Retrieved: 17 January 2021].

[94] http://www.spanishsuccession.nl/naval/battle_silver_fleet_1691.html [Retrieved: 17 January 2021].

[95] Neely, Wayne. (2019). The Greatest and Deadliest Hurricanes to Impact The Bahamas. Indiana: iUniverse. pp.97 – 118.

[96] https://www.tcmuseum.org/projects/molasses-reef-shipwreck [Retrieved: 10 January 2021].

[97] http://digitalcollections.fiu.edu/tequesta/files/1948/48_1_05.pdf [Retrieved: 10 January 2020]. See also:

https://www.jstor.org/stable/pdf/207701.pdf [Retrieved: 10 January 2020].

[98] https://www.britannica.com/biography/Hernan-Cortes [Retrieved: 10 January 2020].

[99] http://digitalcollections.fiu.edu/tequesta/files/1948/48_1_05.pdf [Retrieved: 10 January 2020].

[100] http://digitalcollections.fiu.edu/tequesta/files/1948/48_1_05.pdf [Retrieved: 10 January 2020].

[101] http://digitalcollections.fiu.edu/tequesta/files/1948/48_1_05.pdf [Retrieved: 10 January 2020].

102 http://digitalcollections.fiu.edu/tequesta/files/1948/48_1_05.pdf
[Retrieved: 10 January 2020].

103 https://www.livescience.com/39238-hernan-cortes-conqueror-of-the-aztecs.html [Retrieved 20 May 2020].

104 http://digitalcollections.fiu.edu/tequesta/files/1948/48_1_05.pdf
[Retrieved: 10 January 2021].

105 https://www.history.com/news/st-augustine-first-american-settlement
[Retrieved: 10 January 2021].

106 https://www.orlandosentinel.com/news/os-xpm-2005-10-02-ojimr02-story.html [Retrieved: 10 January 2021].

107 Viele, John. (2001). The Florida Keys: The wreckers. Florida:
Pineapple Press Inc. p.21.

108 Viele, John. (2001). The Florida Keys: The wreckers. Florida:
Pineapple Press Inc. pp.14-15.

109 Woodard, Colin. (2007). The Republic of Pirates: Being the True and
Surprising Story of the Caribbean Pirates and The Man who brought
them down. Florida: Harcourt Inc. p. 1.

110 Las Americas: Ciferri, Alberto (ed,). (An Overview Of Historic And
Socio-Economic Evolution In The Americas. UK: Cambridge Scholars
Publishing. p.309.

111 https://www.britannica.com/topic/Spanish-treasure-fleet [Retrieved:
10 January 2021].

112 https://www.thoughtco.com/etymology-of-hurricane-3080285
[Retrieved: 10 January 2021].

113 https://www.theguardian.com/science/2019/mar/01/spain-logs-shipwrecks-maritime-past-weather-pirates [Retrieved: 10 January 2021].

114 Turnquest, Natasha. (2005). Delimitation of The Maritime Boundary
Between the Commonwealth of The Bahamas and The United States of
America: A Case Study. New York: United Nations-Nippon Sponsorship
Program. pp. 23-24,

115 Markham, Clements R. (1902). *Life of Christopher Columbus.*
Liverpool: G. Philip & Son, Limited. p. 92.

116
https://www.loc.gov/resource/g4980.ar175000/?r=0.165,0.278,0.134,0.05
1,0 [Retrieved 20 May 2020].

117 https://www.britannica.com/technology/Manilla-galleon [Retrieved 10
June 2020].

118 Craton, Michael and Saunders, Gail. (1992). *Islanders in the Stream:
A History of the Bahamian People-From Aboriginal Times to the End of
Slavery.* Georgia: University of Georgia Press. p. 97.

119 https://divingthemaravillas.wordpress.com/ [Retrieved 10 June 2020]

.

[120] https://www.sun-sentinel.com/news/fl-xpm-2013-07-21-fl-golden-madonna-20130722-story.html [Retrieved 10 June 2020].

[121] https://www.washingtonpost.com/archive/politics/1986/11/27/divers-in-bahamas-claim-booty-worth-16-billion/942f472d-1080-4408-8354-67f702924b45/ [Retrieved 10 June 2020].

[122] https://www.sun-sentinel.com/news/fl-xpm-2013-07-21-fl-golden-madonna-20130722-story.html [Retrieved 10 June 2020].

[123] https://www.history.com/news/6-famous-pirate-strongholds {Retrieved 15 September 2021].

[124] https://www.britannica.com/topic/Spanish-treasure-fleet [Retrieved: 10 January 2020].

[125] https://www.theguardian.com/science/2019/mar/01/spain-logs-shipwrecks-maritime-past-weather-pirates [Retrieved: 10 January 2020].

[126] https://www.theguardian.com/science/2019/mar/01/spain-logs-shipwrecks-maritime-past-weather-pirates [Retrieved: 10 January 2020].

[127] https://www.chicagotribune.com/news/ct-xpm-1994-10-02-9410020282-story.html [Retrieved 10 June 2020.

[128] http://www.tribune242.com/news/2021/sep/13/billion-dollar-treasure-exploration-heating/ [Retrieved 15 September 2021].

[129] https://nadl.tamu.edu/index.php/shipwrecks/iberian-shipwrecks/spanish-and-the-new-world/nuestra-senora-de-la-concepcion-1641-2/ [Retrieved 15 September 2021].

[130] https://www.nytimes.com/1979/11/09/archives/the-lost-treasure-of-the-concepcion-sports-of-the-times.html [Retrieved 15 September 2021].

[131] Markham, Clements R. (1902). *Life of Christopher Columbus.* Liverpool: G. Philip & Son, Limited. p. 92.

[132] https://www.loc.gov/resource/g4920.ar177801/?r=0.428,0.048,0.493,0.202,0 [Retrieved: 17 January 2021].

[133] https://www.loc.gov/resource/g4920.ar178102/?r=0.184,-0.034,0.864,0.354,0 [Retrieved: 17 January 2021].

[134] https://blogs.nasa.gov/sailing_with_nasa/tag/florida-straits/ [Retrieved: 17 January 2021].

[135] Marx, Robert, F. (1987). Shipwrecks in the Americas. New York: Dover Publications Inc.p.344.

[136] https://www.encyclopedia.com/places/oceans-continents-and-polar-regions/oceans-and-continents/straits-florida [Retrieved: 17 January 2021].

[137] Singer, D. Steven. (1998). *Shipwrecks of Florida: A Comprehensive Listing.* Florida: Pineapple Press, Inc. p. 13.

[138] https://www.orlandosentinel.com/news/os-xpm-1995-11-12-9511100192-story.html [Retrieved: 17 January 2021].

Bibliography

Aceto, Michael and Williams, Jeffrey Payne. (Eds.). (2003). *Contact Englishes of the Eastern Caribbean*. Amsterdam: John Benjamin Publishing Company.

Barratt, Peter. (2011). *Bahama Saga: The Epic Saga of the Bahama Islands*. Indiana: 1st Books.

Cano, R. (1992). *El español a través de los tiempos*. Madrid: Arco/Libros.

Craton, Michael and Saunders, Gail. (1992). *Islanders in the Stream: A History of the Bahamian People-From Aboriginal Times to the End of Slavery*. Georgia: University of Georgia Press.

Curry, Robert. (1930). *Bahamian Lore*. Paris: (Privately Printed).

Douglass, R. Thomas. (Dec. 1987). The Letter H in Spanish. *Texas: Hispania, 70*(4).

Dunan, Marcel. (1964). *Larousse Encyclopedia of Modern History, From 1500 to the Present Day*. New York: Harper and Row.

Elsayed, R. (2018). *La presencia del arabismo en la antroponimia hispánica contemporánea*. Madrid: Universidad Complutense.

Fernández, Gonzalo de Oviedo y Valdés. (1851). *Historia general y natural de las Indias - Volume 1*. Madrid: La Real Academia De La Historia.

Granberry, Julian and Vescelius, Gary S. (2004). *Languages of the Pre-Columbian Antilles*. Alabama: The University of Alabama Press.

Kamen, Henry. (2005). *Spain 1469–1714* (3rd ed.). New York: Pearson/Longman.

Keegan, William F. and Carlson, Lisabeth A. (2008). *Talking Taino: Caribbean Natural History from a Native Perspective*. Alabama: University of Alabama Press.

Keegan, William F., Hofman, Corinne L. and Rodriguez, Reniel R. (Eds.). (2013). *The Oxford Handbook of Caribbean Archaeology*. Oxford: Oxford University Press.

Little, Benerson. (2007). *The Buccaneer's Realm: Pirate Life on the Spanish Main*. Washington: Potomac Book Inc.

Loven, Sven. (2010). *Origins of the Tainan Culture, West Indies*. Alabama: University of Alabama Press.

Markham, Clements R. (1902). *Life of Christopher Columbus*. Liverpool: G. Philip & Son, Limited.

Mills, Carlton (Ed.). (2008). *A History of the Turks and Caicos Islands*. Oxford: MacMillan Publishers.

Moralejo, A. (1977) *La "J" española y la "J" arábiga: Alfajarín y otros topónimos. Vol. 20-21*. Zaragoza: Archivo de filología aragonesa.

Sauer, Carl Ortwin. (1966). *The Early Spanish Main*. New York: Cambridge University Press.

Singer, D. Steven. (1998). *Shipwrecks of Florida: A Comprehensive Listing*. Florida: Pineapple Press, Inc.

Smith, Jean Reeder and Smith, Lacey Baldwin. (1980). *Essentials of World History*. London: Barron Educational Series.

Spalding, Mark and Bunting, Gillian. (2004). *A Guide to the Coral Reefs of the Caribbean*. California: University of California Press.

Riley, Sandra. (2000). *Homeward Bound: A History of the Bahama Islands to 1850 with a Definitive Study of Abaco In the American Loyalist Plantation Period*. Florida: Riley Hall Publishers.

Sandys, John E. (1910). A Companion to Latin Studies. Chicago: University of Chicago Press.

Other Books By Tellis A. Bethel Sr.

America- A Destiny Unveiled

The Lucayan Story

The Lucayan Islands

The Lucayan Sea (2nd. Ed.)

Trapped On Kooky Island (co-written with Teri M. Bethel)

Author Contact Information

Tellis A. Bethel Sr. Commodore (Ret.) MALIC

P. O. Box CB-11990

Nassau, Bahamas

www.tellisbethel.com

www.lucayansea.com

Email: tbethel@tellisbethel.com

Lightning Source UK Ltd.
Milton Keynes UK
UKHW020616210223
417374UK00010B/1235

9 798401 236944